10653100

SHANKLY
THE LOST DIARY

SHANKLY
THE LOST DIARY

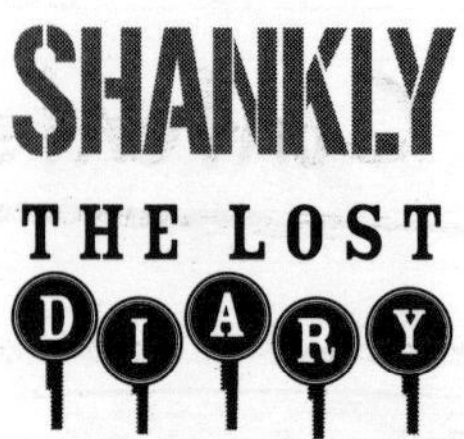

Written by: BILL SHANKLY

Produced by Sport Media, Trinity Mirror North West.
Design & Production: Adam Oldfield
Contributors: Chris McLoughlin, Alan Jewell

Executive Editor: Ken Rogers
Senior Editor: Steve Hanrahan
Editor: Paul Dove
Senior Art Editor: Rick Cooke

First Edition
Published in Great Britain in hardback form in 2013.
Published and produced by Trinity Mirror Sport Media.
PO Box 48, L69 3EB.

All Rights Reserved. No part of this publication may be reproduced, stored in a retrieval system, or transmitted in any form, or by any means, electronic, mechanical, photocopying, recording or otherwise without the prior permission in writing of the copyright holders, nor be otherwise circulated in any form of binding or cover other than in which it is published and without a similar condition being imposed on the subsequent publisher.

Images: Liverpool Echo, Trinity Mirror, PA Photos

ISBN: 9781908695512

Printed and bound in the UK by CPI Group (UK) Ltd, Croydon, CR0 4YY

Contents

"My idea was to build Liverpool into a bastion of invincibility. Napoleon had that idea. He wanted to conquer the bloody world. I wanted Liverpool to be untouchable. My idea was to build Liverpool up and up until eventually everyone would have to submit and give in."

– Bill Shankly's famous quote.
This is the start of that vision...

Foreword by Chris McLoughlin, Editor of The Kop Magazine

Uncovering Shankly's Historic Battle Plan

THE summer of 1962 was notable for a number of reasons.

Brazil became only the second nation to win consecutive World Cups, beating Czechoslovakia 3-1 in the final in Chile of a tournament best remembered for "the battle of Santiago."

In the UK, panda crossings had been introduced on the roads, initially baffling motorists and pedestrians.

A band by the name of the Rolling Stones made their debut at London's Marquee Club while the band of the decade, The Beatles, played their first session at Abbey Road Studios. They preferred to use zebras, rather than pandas, to cross the road.

And on Merseyside, for supporters of both Liverpool and Everton, there was a sense of anticipation in the air. A buzz about what was to come. Thousands were wishing the summer away, itching for the football season to restart.

Evertonians, having seen their side finish fourth, were predicting a title challenge, but for Kopites it felt like an eight-year jail sentence had come to an end. Liverpool Football Club were back in the First Division.

After spending eight seasons in Division Two – and the previous two embroiled in relegation battles, the second of which they failed to survive – a decade of disappointment was finally over. Optimism reigned. Hope had been restored.

Not since 1951 had there been a Merseyside derby in the league, with the 1955 FA Cup 4th round clash the only competitive fixture played between the Reds and their blue brethren in 10 years.

Money-spinning friendlies – known as the Floodlit Cup – had catered for the insatiable Scouse appetite to see Liverpool and Everton clash in the meantime, but it wasn't the real thing. Happily, those days were now gone.

Under the management of Bill Shankly, a Glenbuck-born Scot who was appointed as Liverpool boss in December 1959 having impressed at Huddersfield Town, the Reds had powered their way to promotion.

They topped the table from the first day to last, netted 99 goals, caused a shock in the FA Cup and the Kop had two new heroes – inspirational signings Ian St John and Ron Yeats, the spine of the team.

Shankly had revolutionised the club. He'd wrestled control of team selection from the directors, brought in a new tactical system, trained his team so they were fitter than any other in the division, created Liverpool's first 'Academy' and used the expertise of his backroom staff, like no Anfield boss had ever done before, to detect weakness in opponents.

What's more, he spent the summer of 1962 explaining to readers of Merseyside's leading local newspaper, The Liverpool ECHO, or more specifically, the paper's Saturday evening spin-off title – The Football ECHO, also known as 'The Pink' – exactly how he did it, in unprecedented detail spanning almost 25,000 words.

Launched in 'The Pink' as '*The Hard Road Back*' and revisited here, 50 years later, as '*The Lost Diary*', these entries form a 14-week series that was published after Liverpool had won promotion. Written in his own indomitable style, it was an unusually candid project for Shankly to undertake and was presented to readers in low-key fashion by the paper with a five-paragraph Football ECHO article promoting the series sandwiched in-between the I Zingari League table and a section of the FA Cup final match report.

Indeed, '*The Hard Road Back*' felt like quite a discovery when I stumbled across it in the ECHO archives while, initially, researching an article I was planning to write for The Kop Magazine to mark the 50th anniversary of Liverpool's promotion.

Aside from his autobiography, there isn't a publication out there in which Shankly, speaking in the first person, gives such a detailed account of how he set about restoring the glory days at Anfield.

What makes this all the more exciting is that every word in this book was written before those glory days returned. This isn't Shanks reflecting on the job he did after guiding Liverpool to league championships, FA Cups and the UEFA Cup.

This is Shankly talking in 1962 about a job he felt he was only just starting, without knowing what would transpire when Liverpool returned to the top flight, and taking readers into the Anfield inner-sanctum against his natural instincts. These are his best-laid plans, as they unfolded, and when only the target of promotion had been achieved.

	44	20	10	14	84	53	50
ht	44	22	5	17	81	60	49
m	44	19	11	14	69	70	49
w	44	17	14	13	74	58	48
e	44	20	6	18	79	70	46
m	44	17	12	15	77	70	46
le	44	19	7	18	71	71	45
n	44	18	9	17	61	73	45
fld	44	19	6	19	77	66	44
re	44	20	4	20	70	81	44
rt	44	17	9	18	70	69	43
rt	44	17	9	18	61	71	43
r	44	13	11	20	62	77	37
fld	44	14	9	21	70	87	37
m	44	13	11	20	73	94	37
tr	44	11	7	26	60	85	29
ols	44	8	11	25	52	101	27
er	44	7	12	25	54	96	26

RUGBY LEAGUE

	P	W	D	L	F	A	Pts
	36	32	1	3	985	283	65
d Y	36	32	1	3	822	288	65
stone	36	28	1	7	623	370	57
field	36	25	2	9	494	331	52
gton	36	25	0	11	658	342	50
	36	25	0	11	506	309	50
	36	25	0	11	593	390	50
R.	36	24	0	12	613	450	48
ns	36	23	0	13	606	303	46
	36	22	1	13	643	344	45
	36	21	1	14	527	326	43
rd	36	21	0	15	501	373	42
	36	19	4	13	446	383	42
ton	36	19	2	15	576	435	40
	36	18	3	15	400	334	39
	36	18	1	17	573	415	37
	36	17	0	19	384	497	34
	36	14	1	21	423	558	29
y	36	13	2	21	365	467	28
	36	12	1	23	462	531	25
	36	12	1	23	385	740	25
ven	36	11	2	23	383	539	24
ol B	36	11	1	24	335	600	23
e H	36	9	4	23	317	595	22
	36	10	1	25	354	582	21
	36	9	2	25	255	538	20
ry	36	8	2	26	260	543	18
ter	36	8	1	27	294	668	17
ol C	36	6	0	30	224	753	12
d N	36	5	1	30	288	763	11

CENTRAL LEAGUE

	P	W	D	L	F	A	Pts
	42	30	7	5	115	40	67
ol	42	28	5	9	90	51	61
Villa	42	28	3	11	90	44	59
	42	24	9	9	93	47	57
ey	42	19	10	13	82	63	48
tle	42	20	7	15	82	66	47
r C.	42	19	9	14	80	64	47
	42	19	6	17	95	82	44
n A.	42	18	8	16	69	65	44
d U.	42	17	9	16	84	62	43
r U.	42	18	6	18	88	66	42
sfield	42	19	4	19	73	67	42
W.	42	16	8	18	74	80	40
	42	12	14	16	64	62	38
	42	13	12	17	62	69	38
d W.	42	14	8	20	78	77	36
U.	42	14	8	20	67	93	36
ol	42	12	9	21	68	78	33
C.	42	11	11	20	45	73	33
N.E.	42	8	8	26	49	86	24
r	42	8	8	26	56	135	24
field	42	7	7	28	44	125	21

O-CHESHIRE LEAGUE

	P	W	D	L	F	A	Pts
ch A	34	28	3	3	118	38	59
ch	34	24	4	6	88	42	52
kall	34	20	9	5	86	43	49
n	34	22	3	9	108	[illegible]	47
G.	34	22	3	9	102	[illegible]	47
e	34	19	5	10	94	[illegible]	[illegible]
n T.	34	15	7	12	70	[illegible]	[illegible]
ow A	34	13	9	12	53	[illegible]	[illegible]
U.	34	15	5	14	78	[illegible]	[illegible]
n A.	34	15	3	16	64	[illegible]	[illegible]
A. A	34	11	5	18	56	[illegible]	27
ch A.	34	10	5	19	77	84	25
ch R.	34	11	2	21	58	83	24
Royce	34	7	9	18	[illegible]	85	23
ord	34	8	3	23	[illegible]	120	19
n T R	34	6	6	22	[illegible]	93	18
rd	34	7	4	23	49	128	18
on YC	34	7	3	24	43	95	17

I ZINGARI LEAGUE

DIVISION II

Bootleians	26	19	[illegible]	4	93	45	41
ne's	26	16	[illegible]	5	87	38	37
lle	26	16	[illegible]	5	75	42	37
O.B.	26	15	[illegible]	6	93	33	35
Nalgo	26	14	[illegible]	7	90	44	[illegible]
re	26	13	[illegible]	8	74	80	[illegible]
olts	26	12	[illegible]	12	75	70	[illegible]
e Villa	26	10	[illegible]	11	68	[illegible]	[illegible]
B. O.B.	26	9	[illegible]	12	[illegible]	[illegible]	[illegible]
Trinity	26	8	[illegible]	13	[illegible]	[illegible]	[illegible]
esfield	26	6	[illegible]	14	[illegible]	[illegible]	[illegible]
ey	26	7	[illegible]	15	43	[illegible]	[illegible]
Dale	26	6	[illegible]	17	41	92	[illegible]
eth, OSA	26	1	0	25	31	151	2

WITTON SURPRISE

ttom of the Cheshire gue this season, Witton on caused a surprise last t by beating neighbouring hwich Victoria 2-1 in the l of the Northwich F.A. or Cup before 2,000 spec- s at the Central Ground. on were splendidly led by y, who netted both their s. Rowley replied for hwich.

and Brown did exceptionally well to turn it for a corner.

Burnley just could not seem to get started properly. Already Smith, probably fearing the cramp this pitch can cause so easily, had both stockings down to the ankle.

Norman made a superb tackle to take the ball from Pointer but Pointer won a free kick against White a moment later, and it needed a cheeky reverse header by Blanchflower to his goalkeeper to put a stop to the menace of Miller's free kick.

Jones outspeeded Angus down the left and won a corner after a run of some 50 yards. One way or another Tottenham were sitting pretty, with Greaves almost through from a delightful pass by Smith only to spoil the situation by handling to bring the ball under control.

A clever overhead flick by Pointer from a corner on the right went for nothing and then Blacklaw went to the feet of Smith to push the ball outside the penalty area and tap it back with his foot so that he could pick up without penalty.

Tottenham Link-Up

Burnley kept the ball a little close in attack and Tottenham stepped in to work their close linked progressive moments from full back to half back and so to their own attack.

Jones and Greaves between them almost undid Burnley a second time with a clever interchange that stopped near the six-yard area at the expense of a corner.

Tottenham were now trying to make it an exhibition match, keeping the ball on the floor and moving it smoothly and effectively as though they were determined, come what may, to continue to play their own special brand.

Adamson was the inspiring centre from the left by White.

Out to-day, this unique 32-page ECHO souvenir honours Liverpool's great fight back to Division I. Inside the full colour cover are pages of pictures and articles which tell the Liverpool story over 70 years.

Free with each copy:

FULL COLOUR ART PLATE of the LIVERPOOL F.C. Team.

See your newsagent NOW.

His speed enabled him to get a corner from which Robson made a straight forward header which Brown fielded easily.

Robson then hit a fast centre from the right which somehow contrived to miss every Burnley head. Harris was having a bad time, being scarcely able to put a foot right.

Little had been seen of either White or Medwin so far and when White got a difficult chance close in from a pass by Mackay, he shot all too hastily and very wide.

The tale of Wembley injury continued when Mackay fell heavily and was allowed to lie injured for half a minute while a Burnley attack developed.

Happily Mackay was fit to continue and so the senseless chanting of the Burnley contingent that he should go off, could be ignored.

The combination between the head of Smith and the feet of Greaves was remarkably effective and whatever the solidity of the Burnley defence in normal times it was getting pulled apart this afternoon.

Blacklaw did well to slip away one handed a dangerous

The Hard Road Back—By Bill Shankly

The *Echo* have commissioned Liverpool F.C. manager, Mr. Bill Shankly, to write the "inside" story of his team's hard road back to Division I. The series which will run week by week in the Summer Sports edition, begins a week to-day.

Mr. Shankly, one of football's great characters and perhaps the most forthright man in the game, will trace the championship season from the start telling, as only he can, the drama behind the salient League games and giving his personal story of memorable cup-ties against Preston.

His disclosures, such as the exceptional difficulty the club have had more than once in getting Ronnie Yeats fit for vital games, will make the series one no football fan in the North-West can afford to miss.

Not until Liverpool were "home and dry" in the promotion race would the Liverpool manager write one word of The Hard Road Back.

Now he is doing so the *Echo* Summer Sports edition can help fans re-live all the excitement and drama of a triumphant season in which Mr. Shankly, and his enthusiasm for the game and the club, played such a special part.

Order your Summer Sports edition for the season—TO-DAY!

were always vulner
Burnley blitz of goa
The second half
lack lustre style. On
escape the impres
Tottenham were tak
rather a little
chalantly for their o
My fears for T
were all too well
Harris, the man
done nothing righ
man for once, co
ball smoot and
found Robson
placed to fairly r
home from not
or three yards' ra
That was after 50
The Burnley che
cut short in the
minute when, stra
the re-start, Totte
white moving to c
to centre, foun
standing all alone
to wheel round at
and slam the b
restore Tottenha
miraculously.
Thus, after hal
and none too we
minutes to get an
Burnley found them
better off within
minute.
They might well
to 2-2 if Norman
hooked the be
cleverly when Poin
clean through from
Elder.

Then Cam Raised

When Smith took
the face and lay inj
and Cummings got
tempered with one
there was more
semblance of a rais
happily all was well
recovered.
Smith was not
connect with a mo
centre by Greaves
and in the next mi
Robson putting the
net for the second
from a palpabl
position.
Baker gave Brow
Jones came adrift
first time through h
to pass the ball a
time.
The man of the
me, despite his sid
so far, was the
so far, was the Bu
tain Adamson, wh
put a foot wrong
were making f
blunders in defenc
not being made to
for them.
Norman was as
in the Tottenham
Yeats is at Anfield.

Spurs Not Impress

At this moment
lected a headed cle
flicked in a shot a
over the top.
Pointer was sov
of doubt in the
defence but it
ordinary how m
Burnley came und
middle of move
promise.
Tottenham were

As you will see, he both starts and ends this book by justifying why it was written. It's almost as if he was trying to convince himself it was the right thing to do.

Thankfully, he put aside his caution, because there are some absolute gems in this series of articles. A gold mine of stories that not only give you a real feeling of what life at Anfield was like between 1959 and 1962, but an early insight into Shankly's character.

We're talking about a man who was so desperate to see Liverpool FC win games of football that he tried timing the rate at which the sun set in Sunderland to gain an advantage in terms of which end the Reds should kick towards in the first half! His passion, desire to succeed and the way he was inspired by the famous Kopites comes across loud and clear.

His revelations of how transfer deals were conducted in the boardroom takes you behind the scenes in a way that simply does not happen in modern football, while his explanations on how various logistical headaches were dealt with – such as trying to get back from Norwich when the team bus went missing – captures perfectly what the world of football was like in the early 1960s.

There are some inaccuracies in his recollection

of events compared to statistical records, but bear in mind that this was how Shankly saw things through his own eyes and if he thought one of his players had scored when it was technically an own goal, no-one was going to argue the toss with him!

In 2006, Trinity Mirror Sport Media produced '*The Real Bill Shankly*' with the great man's granddaughter Karen Gill. It sold out. In 2009, we republished Shankly's controversial autobiography more than 30 years after it was launched in 1976. The fans loved it. Now, '*The Lost Diary*' provides a welcome addition to the Shankly collection.

Printed for the very first time since 1962, this is a unique opportunity to read Bill Shankly's personal overview of the Reds' return to First Division football in its entirety. Within two seasons they would be champions of England, and the Reds would embark on a journey that would ultimately see them crowned kings of Europe.

This book provides an early glimpse of the remarkable vision that made it all happen. If you are one of Shankly's disciples, a Liverpool supporter or a football fan in general, I'm absolutely certain you'll enjoy it as much as I did.

*****

I know only too well that Merseyside harbours one of the keenest sets of supporting fans in the country, and also know that out of this wonderful crowd, there are countless thousands whose first love is football, and a passionate love at that.

Why I'm Writing This Diary

When I was approached by the *Liverpool ECHO* to write a series of articles on events at Anfield since my arrival here about two-and-a-half years ago, I finally decided to undertake the commission solely to endeavour to maintain interest in football in Liverpool and district during the close season.

I do not always agree with football reports in this paper and in the normal course of events, have no way of replying to such articles, but as I am now contributing, I feel very strongly that I must take this opportunity of emphasising this fact.

It is not that I resent criticism of my team – indeed I am probably its sternest critic – but I feel criticism can sometimes be too strong. A case in point is the report of the recent match against Everton where the comments make me wonder if the reporter and I were watching the same game.

I know only too well that Merseyside harbours one of the keenest sets of supporting fans in the country, and also know that out of this wonderful crowd, there are countless thousands whose first love is football, and a passionate love at that.

For these people, the summer months are long ones, so it is to them that I am primarily addressing these articles, although I sincerely hope that others who read them will find the same interest in reading them that I find in writing them.

In the course of the series, I shall touch on major and minor events inside the club, the problems of team selection, the little dramas which have been played prior to matches in relation to injured players and how decisions were made regarding a player's fitness.

I shall also deal with my views on a number of matches and incidents in them. Decisions have been taken and announced for which it has not, at the time, been possible to give reasons.

If there are readers who would like my comments on these decisions, or on any controversial points, I shall be only too happy to answer them if they will drop me a line, provided that the answer will not embarrass individuals.

My idea in this matter is to not only enlighten supporters of Liverpool football, but also to help bring those supporters closer together – if that is possible.

A Calculated Risk

After my playing days were over, I served my apprenticeship on the managerial side of football with struggling clubs, but although to call them that may be ungracious, it is a statement of fact and does not detract from my gratitude to them for the opportunity to learn the business.

Then came the chance to come to Liverpool and this is the problem with which I was confronted.

Here was a club which although it had a long spell in Division II, really belonged to the First Division (in my opinion), and it seemed to me that this was my chance of reaching the top and, in doing so, helping to build Liverpool once more into one of the leading clubs in the game.

At the same time I realised that although this was a challenge which everything within me urged me to take up, nevertheless it was a gamble as Liverpool supporters would only accept one thing – success.

I was, at that time, leading as peaceful a life as any football manager can lead in the comparatively sheltered calm of Huddersfield.

Was I to step out of this into the cauldron-like atmosphere of Anfield to undertake a task which, however much I put into it, could end in failure?

Nobody can guarantee success and certainly not quick success, yet it seemed to me that the latter was being demanded and therefore the risk was doubled.

With these thoughts in my mind, I visited Anfield. I talked with the board and I talked with the staff and had a look around the place. I liked what I heard in these conversations and I liked what I saw on my tour of inspection.

From what I had heard and seen, I decided that even if the risk I was taking was great, it was nevertheless a calculated risk and one which I had to take because I am an ambitious man and I knew that the Liverpool club and its supporters were ambitious too. We were therefore sharing a mutual feeling. And so I decided to come to Anfield and arrived here nearly halfway through the season – mid-December 1959.

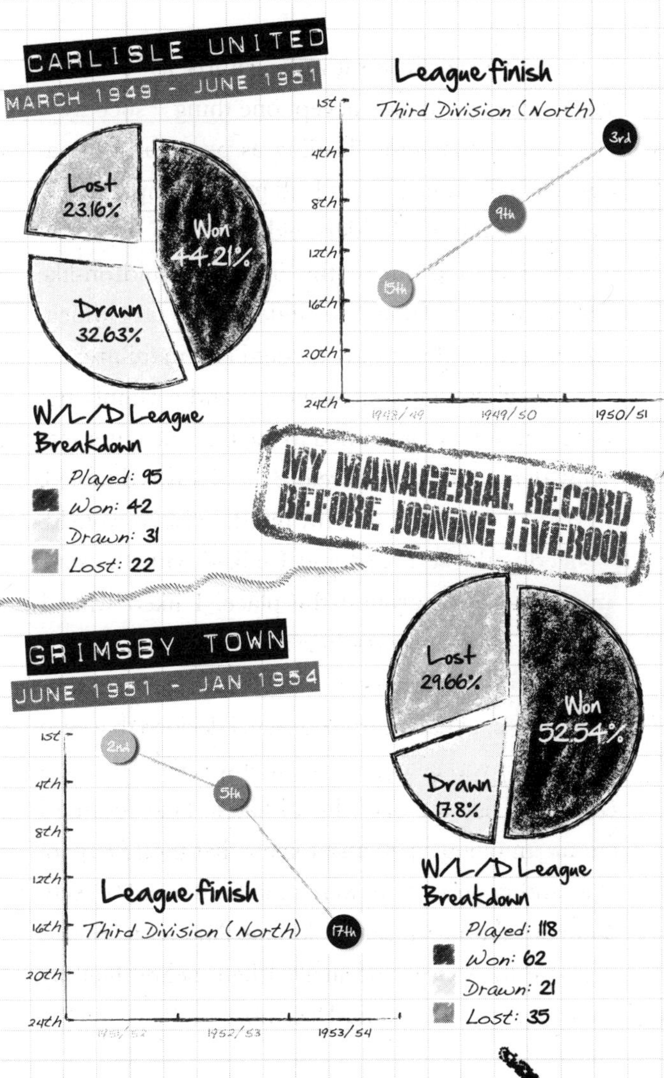
CARLISLE UNITED
MARCH 1949 - JUNE 1951
Lost 23.16%
Won 44.21%
Drawn 32.63%
W/L/D League Breakdown
Played: 95
Won: 42
Drawn: 31
Lost: 22
League finish
Third Division (North)
1st
4th
8th
12th
16th
20th
24th
15th
9th
3rd
1948/49
1949/50
1950/51
MY MANAGERIAL RECORD BEFORE JOINING LIVERPOOL
GRIMSBY TOWN
JUNE 1951 - JAN 1954
League finish
Third Division (North)
2nd
5th
17th
1951/52
1952/53
1953/54
Lost 29.66%
Won 52.54%
Drawn 17.8%
W/L/D League Breakdown
Played: 118
Won: 62
Drawn: 21
Lost: 35

Getting Started

My first task was to assess the possibilities of the club and by this I mean not only the playing strength but also the staff, equipment and all the facilities. Part of the latter was the training ground at Melwood which I had not seen prior to accepting my new post.

I want to put it on record that my first view of it really staggered me with its potential and elated me when I considered its possibilities.

My second task was to talk to the playing and training staff and explain to them what I would demand from them.

Thirdly, I had to see the directors after I had carried out the foregoing and explain to them the support which I would need from them.

I must now acknowledge the ready way in which this support was given, in the same way in which I must acknowledge the support given to me by both the playing and training staff.

As far as assessing the playing strength of the club was concerned, a little consideration will show what a difficult problem faced me.

I had to decide as quickly as possible the needs of the club (if any) before it could be classed as

MY MANAGERIAL RECORD BEFORE JOINING LIVERPOOL

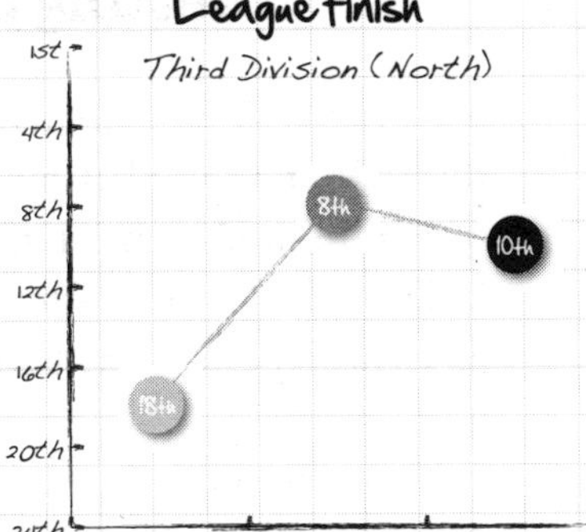

W/L/D League Breakdown

Played: **85**
Won: **35**
Drawn: **23**
Lost: **27**

HUDDERSFIELD TOWN

NOV 1956 - DEC 1959

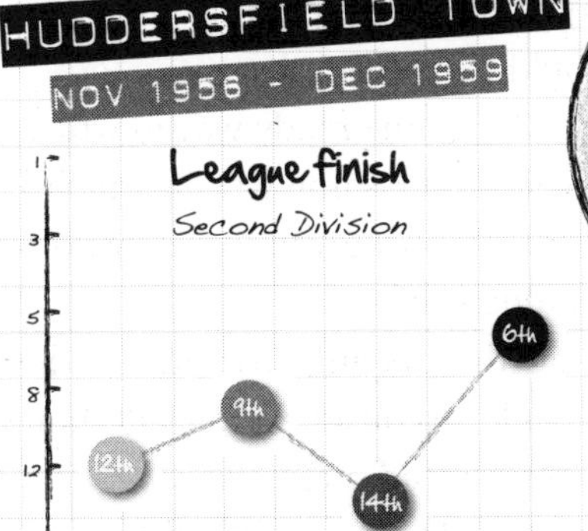

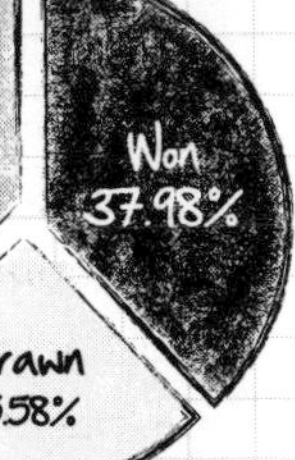

W/L/D League Breakdown

Played: **129**
Won: **49**
Drawn: **33**
Lost: **47**

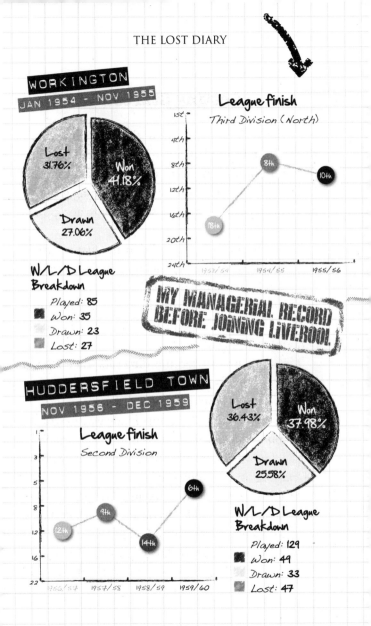

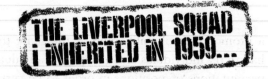

THE LIVERPOOL SQUAD I INHERITED IN 1959...

Player	Position	Age
Doug Rudham	Goalkeeper	33
Bert Slater	Goalkeeper	23
Gerry Byrne	Defender	21
Dick White	Defender	28
Allan Jones	Defender	19
Johnny Molyneux	Defender	28
Ronnie Moran	Defender	25
Geoff Twentyman	Defender	29
John Nicholson	Defender	23
Ian Callaghan	Midfielder	17
Robert Campbell	Midfielder	22
Barry Wilkinson	Midfielder	24
Johnny Wheeler	Midfielder	31
James Harrower	Midfielder	24
Johnny Morrissey	Midfielder	19
Reginald Blore	Midfielder	17
Tommy Leishman	Midfielder	22
Billy Liddell	Midfielder	37
Fred Morris	Midfielder	30
Alan A'Court	Midfielder	25
Dave Hickson	Striker	30
Roger Hunt	Striker	21
Alan Arnell	Striker	26
Jimmy Melia	Striker	22
Alan Banks	Striker	21
Willie Carlin	Striker	19

Average age = $24\frac{1}{2}$ yrs

a promotion probability, and at the same time I had to try individuals and groups of individuals in permutations of positions in order to be certain I had not overlooked anything and was not doing an injustice to anybody.

However, it has always been my policy to get to know my players and so from the start I have trained with them, dined with them, spoke to them daily and all-in-all done everything in my power to be in a position to weigh up accurately their strengths and weaknesses and thus make sure that my assessment of them both as players and as clubmen is correct.

This is something I have always done because in this way, not only can I get to know them thoroughly, but I can also impress on them that what I want from them is a maximum effort from them both in training and on the field of play.

In return, I have always made it clear that they were entitled to expect, and would get from me, a fair deal in every way.

I will be seen, then, that my problem of weighing up the material available was made easier to solve and the time required to solve it shortened by the method which I have described.

A New Way Of Training

As far as the training staff was concerned, I was most fortunate in having a really first class team in Reuben Bennett, Bob Paisley and Joe Fagan, and no praise can be too high for their efforts.

Between us, we set about preparing a plan for improving the training routine and the facilities which at that time existed at Melwood.

We reorganised the whole training system. Every day we conferred and discussed training and before we left for the training ground, every phase and detail was planned so that we could move quickly from one function to another.

We have found it beneficial to train in groups for a number of reasons. Firstly, in this way we can more easily assess the requirements of individuals and secondly we can group together those who require heavier or lighter work.

It may be a new thought to some people that different players require different exercises and quantity of training, but such is the case.

One of the most difficult problems in training a team faces is to size up the requirements of individuals to reach and retain peak fitness.

Does, for instance, a comparatively slightly built

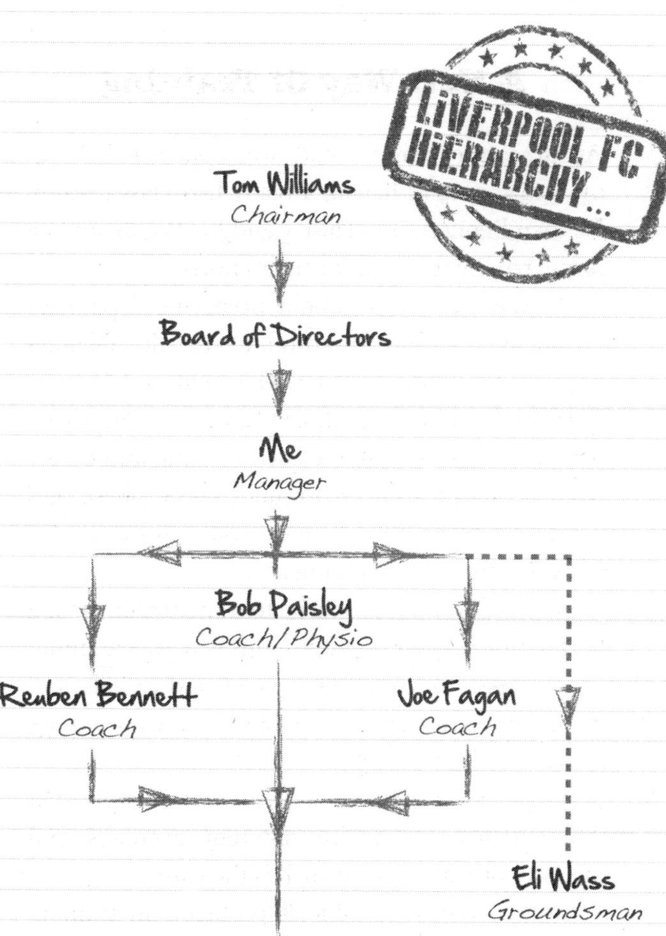
LIVERPOOL FC
HIERARCHY...
Tom Williams
Chairman
Board of Directors
Me
Manager
Bob Paisley
Coach/Physio
Reuben Bennett
Coach
Joe Fagan
Coach
Eli Wass
Groundsman
Playing staff

man like Jimmy Melia require less training than a heavily muscled chap like Ronnie Moran? Or does he require more?

We have found that Moran does not need the amount of work which Melia does, in spite of his size.

This is the sort of problem we have to meet and I mention it only to show that we do everything we can to assess players, not as a whole, but as individuals and work them accordingly.

Nevertheless, you can accept it as fact that every one of them train hard, but get a rest from the grind when we think that a rest is required for their benefit.

You must realise that it is never easy to go 'over the top' in training with staleness resulting. The whole art is to reach fitness and maintain it.

Another aspect of training in which I believe in implicitly is that of tactical talks. In order to remove any misapprehension which you may have about the subject, I want to make it perfectly clear that this does not imply it is my function to stand in front of a blackboard and harangue the lads. A tactical session is more like a good discussion in the Forces with me as the officer leading it.

Just as a good officer realised that he was not the only one present who knew anything about the subject under discussion, so I try to be at a tactical talk.

I start the ball rolling, but anybody who has anything to say knows that he is expected to say it.

When necessary, I become chairman and call the meeting to order, but I have found this method gets results because everyone has his chance of voicing his opinion on any suggestions or move.

If I have emphasised my ideas and the problems with which I had to deal, it is only because I want to make it clear that my whole aim from the start has been to have pre-arranged plans both for training and match play.

*****

"After the way in which we had all trained and worked, this was sheer anti-climax and the club was enveloped in an atmosphere of gloom and dejection."

When I Knew I Had 'Arrived' At Anfield

While I was still finding my way about (literally and metaphorically), the revised training schedule was put into operation, and in this I joined.

This was completely different from the old methods and I must say the boys responded splendidly.

After every training session, we had tactical talks in which we endeavoured to cover everything that could conceivably happen – free-kicks, corners and throw-ins.

We put in a tremendously hard week's work which culminated on the Saturday with a game against Cardiff at Anfield. You can imagine everybody connected with the club was keyed up to a high pitch.

I remember most distinctly the final talk I had with the team prior to the game. In finishing this, I asked them if they had enjoyed the week's work and the unanimous way in which they replied showed the enthusiasm with which they were imbued.

They went onto the field full of the greatest hopes and determination, but during the game they showed the rarest of glimpses of the form of which I knew them to be capable. We lost 4-0.

After the way in which we had all trained and worked, this was sheer anti-climax and the club was enveloped in an atmosphere of gloom and dejection.

It was not that anybody expected a mediocre side suddenly to be transformed into world-beaters as the result of one week under a new manager with new methods, but sheer disappointment having grafted really hard all week, to have been soundly beaten when we fully expected to win.

I went to see the boys while they were still dressing and was greeted by Jimmy Melia. All he said was: "We're sorry, boss. We were too eager to impress."

I am not a demonstrative sort of man, but I could have hugged Jimmy. To hear such sentiments as this, so simply expressed, gave me a feeling of what I can only describe as sympathetic pride.

I was sympathetic because I knew how really hard

SECOND DIVISION
19.12.1959
ANFIELD

Manager		**Manager**	
Bill Shankly		*William Jones*	
LIVERPOOL	0	CARDIFF CITY	4

	Liverpool		Cardiff City
1	Bert Slater	1	Graham Vearncombe
2	Allan Jones	2	Alec Milne
3	Ronnie Moran	3	Ron Stitfall
4	Johnny Wheeler	4	Derek Sullivan
5	Dick White	5	Danny Malloy
6	Robert Campbell	6	Colin Baker
7	Fred Morris	7	Brian Walsh
8	Roger Hunt	8	Derek Tapscott
9	Dave Hickson	9	Graham Moore
10	Jimmy Melia	10	Joe Bonson
11	Alan A'Court	11	Johnny Watkins

Referee:- A Hawcroft
Attendance:- 27,291

Goals:- Tapscott 12, 57
Watkins 34
Bonson 67

they had tried, but this was mixed with a wonderful feeling of pride in being associated with a set of fellows whose first thought, even though terribly disappointment themselves, was to apologise to me for what they considered their own shortcomings.

I knew then that I had 'arrived' at Anfield and had with me a nucleus of players who respected me, were willing to fight for me, and alongside me.

Strengthening The Team

After they had changed, we had a heart-to-heart talk, for by then I had matters in their true perspective.

I told them that this defeat was the best possible thing which could have happened, because in my experience, more is learned from defeats than victories.

I was not prepared to condemn any player on one poor game and we should all be wiser men if we considered what lessons should be learned from what had happened.

We had a post mortem on the game, considering it from every angle, but although what Jimmy Melia had said was perfectly true, it was, in addition, very apparent to me that certain positions needed strengthening.

I then saw the directors and told them the same thing that I had told the players. While there must be a natural feeling of disappointment, any show of gloomy pessimism was quite unwarranted.

This was the Christmas period (the Cardiff game was played on December 19) and we therefore had the usual heavy fixture list immediately in front of us. The next game was on Boxing Day, when we visited Charlton.

We fielded the same team as the one which had lost to Cardiff and although we lost 3-0, there was a great improvement in the standard of play, but, of course, there were weaknesses which had to be remedied. One of these was on the right wing.

The first game I saw at Anfield was a Reserve team game played at the time when I first came to Anfield to look around. This match was against Manchester City Reserves and Liverpool won 5-0.

Jimmy Harrower was in this Reserve side and he had impressed me as a footballer of considerable ability.

He had continued to play some good stuff in the Central League, and I therefore appointed him to the first team as an inside forward to make the best use of the talent available. This enabled me to use Jimmy Melia on the right wing.

It was not my intention that Jimmy should be converted to a winger, because he was, and is, a natural inside-forward, but this was a case of expediency as we really had not wings of sufficient experience among the juniors to play in the senior side.

The plan was for him to be a deep-lying outside right with Roger Hunt playing in the role of poacher at centre-forward alongside Dave Hickson.

This, then, was the revision which I made for the return game against Charlton on December 28, and we were considerably heartened by reversing the result of the Boxing Day game.

I therefore continued with the same line-up and we had the satisfaction of going to Hull for the first game in 1960 and coming away with two points.

A week later we met Leyton Orient in a cup tie at Anfield and once again we were successful. The point I remember about this game was the curious scoring – Roger Hunt got both goals, one a few seconds after the start and the other seconds before the final whistle.

I had, in the meantime, been searching for an outside-right. One possibility was Sammy Reid, then with Motherwell.

He was really an inside-forward but I felt that, on

MAKING MY FIRST TACTICAL CHANGE

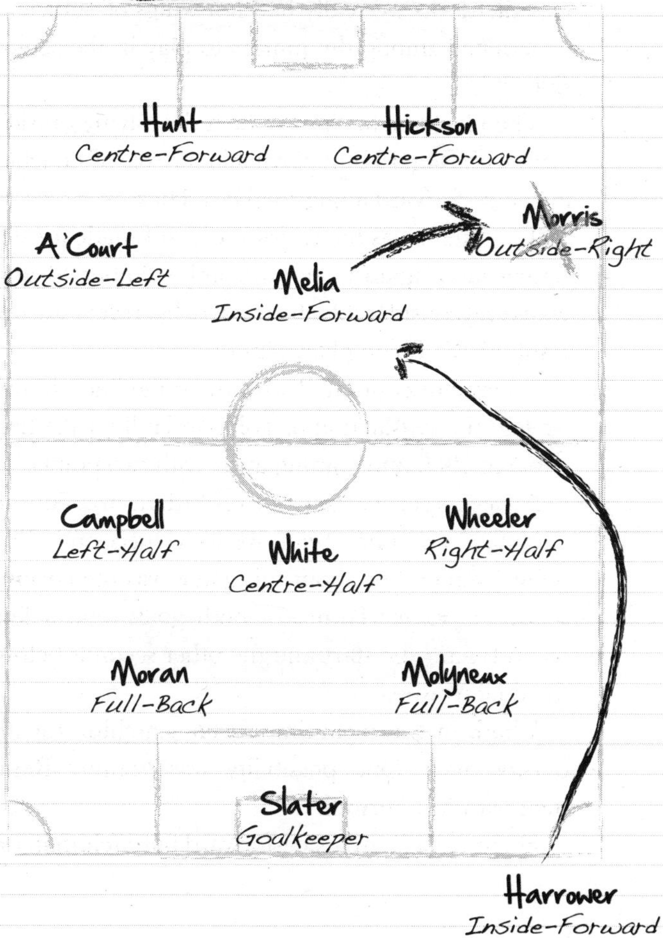

Hunt
Centre-Forward

Hickson
Centre-Forward

~~**Morris**~~
~~*Outside-Right*~~

A'Court
Outside-Left

Melia
Inside-Forward

Campbell
Left-Half

Wheeler
Right-Half

White
Centre-Half

Moran
Full-Back

Molyneux
Full-Back

Slater
Goalkeeper

Harrower
Inside-Forward

AN IMPRESSIVE RUN – SEVEN POINTS FROM FOUR MATCHES

28/12/59	Charlton Athletic A'Court 58, Hunt 63	H	W 2–0	25,658
2/1/60	Hull City Melia 31	A	W 1–0	18,681
16/1/60	Sheffield United Melia 9, Hunt 15, 68	H	W 3–0	33,297
23/1/60	Middlesbrough Thomson 10 (o/g), Hickson 35, Hunt 40	A	D 3–3	28,550

Points won = 7

OUR FA CUP RUN

9/1/60 3rd rnd	Leyton Orient Hunt 1, 90	H	W 2-1	40,343
30/1/60 4th rnd	Manchester United Wheeler 36	H	L 1-3	56,736

account of his small stature, he could be converted into a useful winger without a lot of difficulty.

He did, in fact, come to Liverpool, but only after a short stay was transferred to Falkirk. For the records, he played a big part in Falkirk's promotion.

After Reid decided not to stay with us, the search for suitable talent still continued, but in the meantime I had to make do with the players I had available.

The same team therefore did duty against Sheffield United on January 16. Once again we got two points, winning 3-0 in spite of losing the services of Dave Hickson for part of the game. He got at cross purposes with Coldwell and was sent off.

Our next match was a really wonderful one against Middlesbrough, who played some magnificent football and our own boys matched it, and even surpassed it at times.

At half-time we were leading 3-1, but the opposition pegged us back in the second half and we finished with a 3-3 draw, which was a fitting result to a splendidly fought match.

Thus the introduction of Harrower and the switch of Melia to the wing had shown sustained results as we had obtained seven points out of the last eight possible and in addition had beaten Leyton Orient in a cup tie.

Billy And Cally

The following week brought this minor run of success to an end when we were knocked out of the cup by Manchester United, without being disgraced.

It had become apparent, however, that Jimmy Melia was not happy on the wing. He lost his form and his place in the team.

We still had been unable to find the winger who would satisfy my requirements and with no youngster of sufficient experience available, I brought back Billy Liddell to fill the outside-right position for the game at Plymouth.

This match notched another point and Billy continued on the right for another 10 games. He was long past the age when most players have hung up their boots and the edge had gone from his speed, but he still retained his zest for the game and continued to delight his thousands of fans by his presence in the side.

However, as I knew and as Billy knew, this was not the answer to our problem, but he did fill the position for this period and during it young Ian Callaghan had been continually bringing himself to my notice by his good displays in the Reserve side.

Such consistency brought his reward when I

Callaghan/Liddell
Right Wing

Hunt
Centre-Forward

Hickson
Centre-Forward

Melia
Outside-Right

A'Court
Outside-Left

Harrower
Inside-Forward

Campbell
Left-Half

White
Centre-Half

Wheeler
Right-Half

Moran
Full-Back

Molyneux
Full-Back

Slater
Goalkeeper

Byrne
Full-Back

introduced him to senior football for the game against Bristol Rovers at the age of 17. This game was won 4-0 and he retained his place for the last five games of which we won four and drew the other.

In Callaghan, I felt that we had a youngster who showed real promise of becoming a Liverpool player of the future. At the time he was really not ready for big time football, but the experience which he had gained had been invaluable to him.

This brought me to the end of my first half-season with the club. We finished third once again, just missing that coveted promotion.

In spite of Callaghan's promise, I felt that a more experienced winger was a necessity and in reviewing the games since my arrival, I became more than ever convinced that my earlier assessment of the club's strength was correct.

In spite of our excellent finish, I knew that we fell a long way short of being a championship team.

*****

	Team	P	W	D	L	F	A	Pts
1	Aston Villa	42	25	9	8	89	43	59
2	Cardiff City	42	23	12	7	90	62	58
3	Liverpool	42	20	10	12	90	66	50
4	Sheffield United	42	19	12	11	68	51	50
5	Middlesbrough	42	19	10	13	90	64	48
6	Huddersfield Town	42	19	9	14	73	52	47
7	Charlton Athletic	42	17	13	12	90	87	47
8	Rotherham United	42	17	13	12	61	60	47
9	Bristol Rovers	42	18	11	13	72	78	47
10	Leyton Orient	42	15	14	13	76	61	44
11	Ipswich Town	42	19	6	17	78	68	44
12	Swansea Town	42	15	10	17	82	84	40
13	Lincoln City	42	16	7	19	75	78	39
14	Brighton & H A	42	13	12	17	67	76	38
15	Scunthorpe United	42	13	10	19	57	71	36
16	Sunderland	42	12	12	18	52	65	36
17	Stoke City	42	14	7	21	66	83	35
18	Derby County	42	14	7	21	61	77	35
19	Plymouth Argyle	42	13	9	20	61	89	35
20	Portsmouth	42	10	12	20	59	77	32
21	Hull City	42	10	10	22	48	76	30
22	Bristol City	42	11	5	26	60	97	27

"I must have covered several thousand miles in my search for talent, not only for our immediate needs, but also for Liverpool teams of the future."

The First Liverpool Academy

We had been interested in a number of players, but it had not been possible to do business with their clubs. In the interim period, I had to use the playing strength available.

Out of a number of players I had seen during the season (and do not read into this that they were all wingers because I have mentioned a right-wing weaknesses), Kevin Lewis had attracted my attention as a player who had shown a great goalscoring potential with Sheffield United and we obtained his services during the close season.

Unfortunately, this was the only signing we were able to make in the transfer market with a view to the immediate strengthening of our weakness.

I must, however, have covered several thousand miles in my search for talent, not only for our immediate needs, but also for Liverpool teams of the future.

A first class nursery is an essential for any club and I brought to Anfield a number of boys who attracted my attention as youngsters out of the ordinary.

These included James McKenzie, a full-back from Stirlingshire. Robert Graham, outside-right (Motherwell). George Scott, an inside-forward from Aberdeen. Another inside-forward, Gordon Wallace from Glasgow. An outside-left from Dundee, Philip Tinney. And a Liverpool schoolboy wing-half, Tommy Smith.

All these boys have been kept and I regard them as youngsters of the highest promise.

Five out of the six are from Scotland and from this you must not infer that I did not have a look at the English lads, nor must you think that there was a dearth of talent in England. Neither of these statements would be true.

There is plenty of talent in England and I see it, but the reason that nothing was done in the matter was the fierce competition for these English lads. Probably one of the factors was that we were a Second Division club at the time competing with top class clubs from Division One.

Players In

MF	Kevin Lewis	Sheffield United	£13,000	06-1960
MF	Gordon Milne	Preston NE	£16,000	08-1960
FW	Alf Arrowsmith	Ashton United	£1,250	08-1960

Outgoings = £30,250

Players Out

GK	Doug Rudham	J'burg Ramblers	Free	05-1960
MF	Fred Morris	Crewe Alexandra	£4,000	06-1960
MF	Reginald Blore	Southport	Free	07-1960
MF	Barry Wilkinson	Bangor City	£5,000	08-1960

Income = £9,000

Academy Additions

DF	James McKenzie	Stirlingshire	Free
MF	Robert Graham	Motherwell	Free
FW	George Scott	Aberdeen	Free
FW	Gordon Wallace	Glasgow	Free
MF	Philip Tinney	Dundee	Free
DF	Tommy Smith	Liverpool Schoolboys	Free

Why Can't Liverpool Sign Players?

This may be an opportune moment to make a few remarks on this question of transfers. It is impossible not to know that our supporters have had (and have) strong feelings on the question of where our weaknesses lay (or lie).

If one were to accept all the points of view expressed in public, then one would be faced with the absurd position of providing almost a completely new team. When all is said and done, only those on the inside of a club know all the facts.

How often has it been said: "Other clubs can buy these players, why can't Liverpool?" The true answer to a question of this sort may be any one of a number.

The player might not fill a position we consider to be weak. He might not, in our opinion, fit in with the style of play we were attempting. The figure asked might be in far excess of our value of his worth. He might be a good enough footballer but not the type of man whom we cared to employ.

Or we might agree terms with a club for a player we wanted, only to find that his wife would be prepared to live anywhere in the British Isles except Merseyside!

It will be seen that a transfer is governed by a number of factors. If a cheque for £250,000 or more is to be spent, all the factors must be most carefully considered so that the player will in return pay dividends one way or the other.

A Costly Injury

We put in a very strong pre-season training programme. This was started a little earlier than usual because the club had entered a competition known as the Friendship Cup, which was competed for by both English and French teams.

We had been drawn against Nantes and we flew there. I had made two changes from the side which concluded the previous season in a successful manner.

Naturally, I played Kevin Lewis as a new signing instead of Callaghan, and in addition brought in Gerry Byrne at right-back in place of Johnny Molyneux. The team played exceedingly well against very strong opposition and we won 2-0.

This victory was marred by one unfortunate accident. Roger Hunt received an ankle injury and although he opened with the team for our

Friendship Cup – 1st Leg
Stade Marcel Saupin
Attendance: 3,000
Date: 11.08.1960

Hunt
Centre-Forward

Hickson
Centre-Forward

Lewis
Outside-Right

A'Court
Outside-Left

Melia
Inside-Forward

Leishman
Left-Half

Wheeler
Right-Half

White
Centre-Half

Moran
Full-Back

Byrne
Full-Back

Slater
Goalkeeper

Nantes 0 Liverpool 2

Goals: Hunt 39
Lewis 67

initial league fixture, it was soon obvious that the injury which he had sustained was more than the bruising which was first diagnosed.

As it turned out, his ankle troubled him throughout the rest of the season, and in consequence he was forced to miss a lot of matches.

In the later stages of the season, he had a long spell out of the game. It will thus be seen that we paid a high price for our win against Nantes.

Introducing The 3-3-4 Formation

For a team with promotion aspirations, we opened the season in a deplorable fashion. The first match was at home, against Leeds, and this marked the league debut of Lewis for Liverpool.

He celebrated it with a solid display and scored a clever goal which he paved the way for himself. That was two points in the bag, but I could not help feeling the win should have been more clear cut and convincing against a side that was not very strong.

On the following Wednesday, we played Southampton (away) and found them a side

SECOND DIVISION
20.08.1960
ANFIELD

Manager Bill Shankly		Manager Jack Taylor	
LIVERPOOL	2	LEEDS UTD	
1	Bert Slater	1	Ted Burgin
2	Gerry Byrne	2	Jimmy Ashall
3	Ronnie Moran	3	Alf Jones
4	Johnny Wheeler	4	Eric Smith
5	Dick White	5	Jack Charlton
6	Tommy Leishman	6	Freddie Goodwin
7	Kevin Lewis	7	Billy Bremner
8	Roger Hunt	8	Don Revie
9	Dave Hickson	9	John McCole
10	Jimmy Melia	10	Peter Fitzgerald
11	Alan A'Court	11	Colin Grainger

Goals:- Lewis 28
Hickson 35

Attendance:- 43,041

which served up some really first class football, which emphasised what I had thought about our performance in the Leeds game.

We were thrashed 4-1 and that is an expression I use with the greatest reluctance. Possibly the margin of their win was affected by a groin injury to Gerry Byrne during the course of the game, but I do not want to detract from their performance, which was of the highest order.

The injury kept Gerry out of the game against Middlesbrough and Johnny Molyneux was brought back as his deputy. The best we could manage was a 1-1 draw.

A few days later we met Southampton in the return at Anfield and they confirmed their superiority. Thus, out of the first eight possible points we had scraped a miserable three.

After the finish which we had put in at the end of the previous season, this was a disappointing and discouraging start; something had to be devised to adapt those players which we had.

The scheme we brought into operation was based on the fact that Harrower was essentially a good footballer, but for a forward, was not the best of attacking players.

We therefore brought him in at a position

which was shown as inside-left in the programme, alongside Alan A'Court (or occasionally alongside John Morrissey because we sometimes interchanged the position of the two wings).

I have purposely said that the programme showed Harrower as inside-left, but I felt that this lack of thrust made him more suitable for a position which could be described as a semi-half-back.

He would have the function of lying much further back than is usual for an inside-forward, thus drawing his opposing half-back out of place and from this position playing either Tommy Leishman or Johnny Wheeler with the ball as they moved forward.

He would then temporarily replace either of them as a defensive player and they would supply the drive and support which the forward line so badly needed.

This plan forced the wing-halves to attack far more than I normally like, but personal preferences of this kind had to go by the board if the idea was to be successfully operated.

Thus was born at Anfield the plan which we refereed to as 3-3-4. At that time, I know many people were offering the criticism that the wing-

Hunt
Centre-Forward

Hickson
Centre-Forward

Harrower
~~Inside-Forward~~

A'Court
Outside-Left

Lewis
Outside-Right

defend

defend

attack

attack

Semi-Half-Back

Leishman
Left-Half

Wheeler/Milne
Right-Half

White
Centre-Half

Moran
Full-Back

Byrne/Molyneux
Full-Back

Slater
Goalkeeper

halves were attacking too much; now they know the reason.

They also know that I am in agreement with them – in theory. There is one great argument both against their criticism and my dislike of overdoing the attacking functions of the wing-halves, and that is that the plan worked!

When Harrower played his part competently, the scheme was so effective that we moved from the dismal groove in which we had started into one in which we had a run of 14 games without defeat. We had, by Christmas, run into a challenging position in spite of our dreadfully poor start to the season.

For all this time, Jimmy Melia was languishing in the background and feeling most unsettled about his position, which was very understandable in the case of such a talented player.

However, he knew the position in which we had been and from which we were emerging and I was able to assure him that he would get his place in the side again when we were in a position to play an orthodox game.

We had, during this run of success, moved into second position in the table, only four points behind Sheffield United with a couple of games in hand.

SECOND DIVISION
15.04.1961
CARROW ROAD

Manager Archibald Macaulay		**Manager** Bill Shankly	
NORWICH CITY	2	LIVERPOOL	
1	Sandy Kennon	1	Bert Slater
2	Bryan Thurlow	2	John Molyneux
3	Ron Ashman	3	Gerry Byrne
4	Roy McCrohan	4	Johnny Wheeler
5	Barry Butler	5	Dick White
6	Matt Crowe	6	Tommy Leishman
7	George Waites	7	Kevin Lewis
8	Brian Whitehouse	8	Roger Hunt
9	Terry Allcock	9	Dave Hickson
10	Jimmy Hill	10	Jimmy Melia
11	Bill Punton	11	Johnny Morrissey

Goals:- Whitehouse, Hill

Goal:- Hickson

Attendance:- 21,204

	Team	P	W	D	L	F	A	Pts
1	Ipswich Town	42	26	7	9	100	55	59
2	Sheffield United	42	26	6	10	81	51	58
3	Liverpool	42	21	10	11	87	58	52
4	Norwich City	42	20	9	13	70	53	49
5	Middlesbrough	42	18	12	12	83	74	48
6	Sunderland	42	17	13	12	75	60	47
7	Swansea Town	42	18	11	13	77	73	47
8	Southampton	42	18	8	16	84	81	44
9	Scunthorpe United	42	14	15	13	69	64	43
10	Charlton Athletic	42	16	11	15	97	91	43
11	Plymouth Argyle	42	17	8	17	81	82	42
12	Derby County	42	15	10	17	80	80	40
13	Luton Town	42	15	9	18	71	79	39
14	Leeds United	42	14	10	18	75	83	38
15	Rotherham United	42	12	13	17	65	64	37
16	Brighton & HA	42	14	9	19	61	75	37
17	Bristol Rovers	42	15	7	20	73	92	37
18	Stoke City	42	12	12	18	51	59	36
19	Leyton Orient	42	14	8	20	55	78	36
20	Huddersfield Town	42	13	9	20	62	71	35
21	Portsmouth	42	11	11	20	64	91	33
22	Lincoln City	42	8	8	26	48	95	24

However, our period of prosperity came to an end by Rotherham United beating us 1-0, and from that point to the end of the season, we played indifferently, losing a number of games which we might have been expected to win.

By mid-April we were lying third to Ipswich and Sheffield United, but our visit to Norwich, to whom we lost 1-2, virtually put an end to any real hopes of moving up at the end of that season. We were in the position of waiting for those above us to make mistakes.

As history shows, this they did not do and so once again we were bridesmaids; our splendid supporters must have wondered if the time would ever arrive when we would be the bride.

*****

"What was lacking was a man of experience to occupy the centre-forward position, a player who could play football, create openings, score goals, and at the same time hold the line together."

How I Signed Ian St John

I felt we had achieved as much as we had without really having the talent in certain positions to take the side into the First Division and, not only that, to make a good show when we got there.

As much as anything, I was desperately sorry for the team. No-one could have fought harder or given more.

If you give everything you have and it is not enough, you cannot be blamed for failure.

The team had done this and if some of them fell short because of their own limitations of what was required, then I could not reasonably find fault with them but only commiserate.

Any fault (if it can be so termed) for our failure lay in the fact that there were weaknesses of which we knew, but had not been able to remedy. The forward line was one of my concerns; it was so nearly a very good one and yet I knew it did not function as it should.

We had a choice of A'Court, Lewis, Callaghan and Morrissey as wingers, and Melia, Hunt, Hickson and Harrower (until the latter was transferred to Newcastle in March) from which to choose for the inside positions.

We had tried these players in different combinations of positions but always it came back to the same situation – we had five men without a leader.

What was lacking was a man of experience to occupy the centre-forward position, a player who could play football, create openings, score goals, and at the same time hold the line together.

This was a lot to ask of any individual. Those who I knew with these qualifications were settled with clubs which were not prepared to part with such a precious jewel.

I had discussed this matter with the board and they were in complete agreement with my views. I knew that when the possibility arose of signing

Outside attack

Player	Position	Last season Games	Goals
Alan A'Court	Outside-Left	37	7
Kevin Lewis	Outside-Right	36	22
Ian Callaghan	Outside-Right	5	0
Johnny Morrissey	Outside-Left	24	5

Inside attack

Player	Position	Last season Games	Goals
Jimmy Melia	Inside-Right	27	3
Roger Hunt	Centre-Forward	36	19
Dave Hickson	Centre-Forward	38	17
James Harrower	Inside-Left	25	9

the right man for this position, then the matter of putting it to the directors was a mere formality.

On Sunday morning, April 30, I happened to see a paragraph in a Scottish paper which indicated that Ian St John had said he wanted to leave Motherwell.

Now St John was one of my list of players who had the qualifications which I was certain would weld our forwards into a real attacking force.

I had seen him in action in many games, among which were the Scottish league against the English league, Scotland against England and the Scottish Second Division team against a Scottish Selected side.

In these games he had appeared against such centre-halves as Tony Knapp, Peter Swan and last but by no means least our very own Ronnie Yeats – although he was not ours at that time. Any players who could more than hold his own against opposition of such calibre was the man for me.

I had often seen reports of this sort about various players before, only to find that they were figments of someone's imagination, on inquiry, to find that any difference between a player and his club which had existed had been smoothed over.

First thing on Monday morning, I saw my chairman, Mr T.V. Williams, and told him of what

I had seen. At his suggestion I telephoned the Motherwell club and spoke to their manager, Bobby Ancell.

After disappointments in the past over this sort of inquiry, I was quite prepared for another, but on this occasion I was greeted with the news that what I had seen in the paper was correct, the item was the first that had been published and that the evening papers would contain the news that the Motherwell club was prepared to consider offers for this player.

I was also given information that Motherwell had a local cup fixture against Hamilton 'Accies' the same evening and that St John would be playing.

Within two hours, a party consisting of the chairman, the vice-chairman (Mr S. C. Reakes) and myself were on our way north.

A Tug-O-War Until Past Midnight

We arrived at the Motherwell ground in time for the game and found that St John was to play in an inside-forward position. As for the game, the Accies were a poor side, providing little real opposition, so we saw an uninteresting match.

However, we were there to buy this player and not to assess his qualities. I had watched this player for nearly two years and was only waiting for him to come into the market. It was now or never.

After the match, the Motherwell board and the Liverpool party commenced their discussion. This was about 9.30pm.

As soon as we informed the Motherwell directors that we had a concrete interest in St John, a message was sent to him telling him of the situation and asking him not to leave the ground.

The talks were carried out in a most friendly, but businesslike atmosphere. We told them we definitely wanted St John and, in turn, they gave us a figure which they said could be considered as a basis for negotiation.

From this point, discussion went on for an hour or more and then the Liverpool party was requested to leave the room for a short time while the Motherwell board conducted a private discussion.

After being invited back once more, bargaining continued for some time until we felt that we, in turn, ought to have a private talk among ourselves so that we could exchange views on how each of us considered matters were progressing.

IAN ST JOHN SCOUT REPORT

Position: *Inside-Forward/ Centre-Forward*
Birthplace: *Motherwell*
Age: *22yrs 7mnths*
Height: *5ft 8ins*

Club Career

Motherwell: 1957 – present
Debut: *Nov 1957 v Queen of the South*
League Appearances: 113
League Goals: *80*

International Career

Scotland: 1959 – present
First Cap: *May 5 1959 v West Germany*
Senior Appearances: *7*
Senior Goals: 1

Previous Clubs: *Motherwell Bridge Works, North Motherwell, Douglas Water Thistle*

Notable achievements

* *Hat-trick in 2mins 30secs v Hibernian (Aug 15, 1959).*
* *Six goals in 9–2 friendly win v Flamengo (Apr 26, 1960).*

Expected fee – £37,500
Proposed wage – £30 week

Accordingly, we asked to be left to ourselves and our hosts left the room. We then carried out our own personal assessment of the situation, and having done this, the meeting continued once more. In this way, the tug-o-war dragged on until well past midnight, and eventually agreement was reached.

While all this was going on, Ian St John and his wife had been waiting patiently in another room, and it is not difficult to imagine their feelings as time dragged on without news from the parties whose deliberations could have such an effect on their whole future.

When you are in the dentist's waiting room, eventually your turn must come and so it must have seemed to Ian as we talked.

Naturally, we kept them in suspense for as short a time as possible, so immediately when we reached agreement, we informed them.

The Motherwell directors had now completed their part of the transaction; we had the most delicate part still to do and that was to persuade this great little player and his wife that it would be in their interests to come to Liverpool.

Actually, this was not as difficult as the earlier part of the night had been and we agreed with them that they would travel back to Merseyside the following day.

Up to this time, although I had taken part in a large number of transfers in my capacity as managers of different clubs, the greatest amount of money which had changed hands as a result of any one signature was £4,000.

I am not at liberty to disclose the amount we paid for St John. I can say it made my previous top figure look very small indeed and it was a record fee for Liverpool.

Bette St John Has The Final Say

We met the St Johns as arranged the following morning and found them in some state of indecision. This, to me, was understandable, because the step they were contemplating was a very big one.

I suppose that they had discussed the matter and wondered if it might not be wiser to wait and see if another offer would be forthcoming from some club less remote from south-west Scotland than Merseyside.

The idea of their coming to Liverpool was

so that they could have a look at the place and consider what we had to offer in the way of accommodation and we pointed out that even if they eventually decided not to come, they had nothing to lose by making this preliminary visit.

On this basis, we set off by road and arrived at Anfield late in the afternoon. A board meeting had been convened and was in progress and a full report of the steps taken was made to the directors.

St John was introduced to the members of the board and then whisked away by car with Mrs St John to view the particular house we had in mind for them.

My male readers will understand my relief when they returned with the news that Bette St John was extremely pleased with what was to be her future home.

This left us with the formality of the player considering signing-on terms, which, after a brief discussion, he accepted.

At this junction it might be appropriate that, at the time that St John arrived, the wage structure in the game had been altered so that a maximum wage had been abolished and in accordance with this, the wage scale at Anfield had been adjusted.

We informed St John that we were offering him

exactly the same pay as that which the nucleus of the team were receiving and that nobody was being paid more.

This assurance satisfied him at once and he signed without hesitation.

*****

"I saw Yeats as possibly another George Young of the future and certainly the man to weld our defence together in the way St John could weld the forwards."

From Benny Hill To Big Ron Yeats

Our signing of Ian St John was to the great satisfaction of everybody at Anfield. I felt we had secured a player who would knit together our forward line and from the somewhat disunited group of individuals which it had been, transform it into a real attacking force.

I ought to add that several clubs besides Liverpool were keenly interested in St John, and I believe that if we had not been on the spot when we were, then he would now certainly be playing for some other English club.

Without the initial bit of good luck which allowed my eye to light upon that paragraph in a Scottish paper, we could not have travelled to Motherwell in time to undertake the negotiations which led to his signature, but at the same time I have to acknowledge the chairman's prompt reaction to the news.

As these articles constitute a history of what took place at Anfield from the time I took over the management, and as I have given in detail the events leading to the signing of St John, it is logical to record what are, at the moment, lesser signings but any or all of which may turn out to be stars of the future.

About this time, then, the following 15-year-olds came to Anfield on the ground staff – Alec Totten, full-back, an amateur. Benny Hill, outside-left. Joe Parley, centre-half and John Bennett, wing-half.

Because we have put these boys on the staff, it can be inferred that we have a high opinion of their present ability and promise for the future, although nobody can tell how any player will develop.

The New Deal

I mentioned last week that St John came to Anfield at a time when the 'new deal' for the players had just come into being and it might not be out of place at this point to enlighten those readers who may not be aware exactly what this implied.

Players In

MF	Ian St John	Motherwell	£37,500	05-1961
MF	Ron Yeats	Dundee United	£22,000	07-1961

Outgoings = £59,500

Players Out

MF	Robert Campbell	Wigan Athletic	£1,000	1961
FW	Alan Arnell	Tranmere Rovers	Free	02-1961
MF	James Harrower	Newcastle United	£15,000	03-1961
FW	Alan Banks	Cambridge City	£3,000	1961
FW	Dave Hickson	Cambridge City	£1,000	07-1961
DF	John Nicholson	Port Vale	£2,000	08-1961

Income = £22,000

Academy Additions

DF	Alec Totten	Free
FW	Benny Hill	Free
DF	Joe Parley	Free
MF	John Bennett	Free
GK	William Molyneux	Free

There had been certain points of contention between the Players' Union on the one hand and the Football League management committee on the other.

Over a period of years, negotiations had taken place between the two parties with the result being that the lot of the player had gradually been improved.

One of the major points of issue had been the question of the maximum wage, and it is fair to say that professional footballers owe a lot to Jimmy Hill, their secretary at that time, for his able negotiations on their behalf.

The maximum wage had been abolished and, in addition, agreement had been reached over longer contracts and the establishment of a Benevolent Fund, so that the efforts of professional footballers were being well recognised.

One point of issue, and a major aim of the Players' Union, has been freedom of contract, but much as I am in favour of improved conditions for players, at the same time these conditions must also improve the game.

The granting of free contracts, in my opinion, is against the game's best interests and is something with which I cannot agree.

GOODWILL DRAMA

AN UNEASY truce is the ... meeting between ... at the Mini...

By BILL HOLD...

at today's ... sentatives

ABOLITION OF THE MAXIMUM WAGE

...leads his 'team' to victory . . . and the right to freedom

HILL'S HOUR OF TRIUMPH

By BILL HOLDEN and KEN JONES

THIS was Jimmy Hill's hour of triumph. The bearded Fulham inside forward, chairman of the Professional Footballers' Association, finally led his team to victory—the right to freedom—yesterday.

His eight-month battle with the Football League chiefs to end the players' "slave" contract was finally won in a four-hour meeting at the Ministry of Labour.

Immediately it was over Hill read an official statement from his management committee hailing the new agreement with the League as "an historic moment for football in this country.

"We have reached an honourable agreement which must eventually be of benefit to the players, the League, the public and football itself."

Hill then appealed to players to give the new system their wholehearted support.

'Not Easy'

League agree to end the Soccer 'slave' contract

Peace terms

1. No transfers to take place du... term of the contract, except b... consent of club and player.
2. Players to be informed by May ... ing the end of the contract of ... wish for new contract.
3. Player to decide by May 31 ... not to accept.
4. If he does not accept, the club ... and place him on the transfer...
5. If he is not transferred by Ju... club may continue to retain h... ment of £15 per week in First D... Second Division, £13 Third Division, ... Division up to July 31.
6. If not transferred by July 3... will sign a monthly contr... offered terms, subject to the club... efforts to transfer him.
7. If by August 31 he is still no... the Management Committee ... ball League will, on the applic... player, deal with the matter. T... also retain the present right to ... Management Committee in co... transfer fees, etc., at any time.

IMPORTA... ANNOUNCEM... FROM EMPI...

THIS WEEK

SEND YOUR USUAL

WHICH HAS THE FULL

ENGLISH & SCOTTISH

SATURDAY'S MATC...

BE PLAYED AS

Daily Mirror

STAR STUDDED BRIDE!

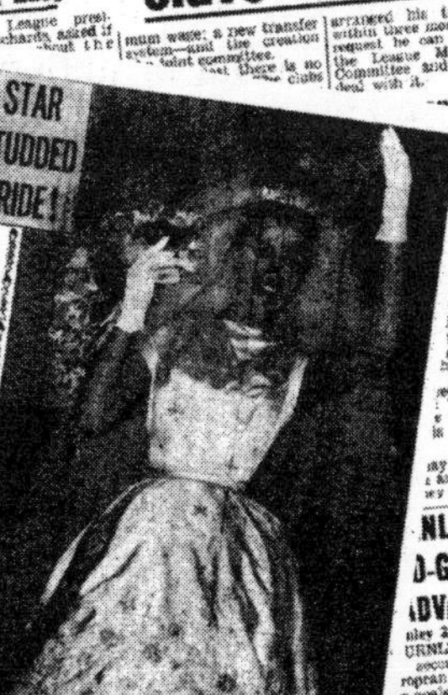

SOCCER STRIKE STARTS JAN 14

THE Soccer strike is ON. First games affected ... be Football League match...

...NLEY GRAB ...-GOAL CUP ADVANTAGE

During 19...

ZETT...

originators of 1/4...

the highest top

We at Liverpool had started the 'new deal' by offering all first-team players the same wage, which seems to have worked well so far. Other clubs have varied wage salaries for different categories of players, a policy which could have all sorts of complications.

Apart from informing any readers who did not know what the deal involved, I have written about it in some length so that readers may know how it affects the Liverpool club.

In return for the better conditions of employment, clubs and the public are entitled to an all-out effort from the players; the boys at Anfield have unquestionably given this during the recent season.

St John Off The Mark And Ron On The Radar

As for St John himself, he and his wife moved to Liverpool and he made his debut at Goodison Park against Everton and what a storybook debut this turned out to be.

There was the usual vast crowd for this 'derby' game and whether they were our own supporters

Liverpool Senior Cup Final
Goodison Park
Attendance: 51,669
Date: 09.05.1961

Hunt
Centre-Forward

St John
Centre-Forward

Callaghan
Outside-Right

Morrissey
Outside-Left

Melia
Inside-Forward

Milne
Left-Half

Wheeler
Right-Half

White
Centre-Half

Byrne
Full-Back

Molyneux
Full-Back

Slater
Goalkeeper

Everton 4 Liverpool 3

St John 43,
St John 50,
St John 89

or supporters of our friends across the park, they were all treated to a display of centre-forward play of the highest class.

He scored a hat-trick, but this was only incidental to the life and fire which he brought to the forwards. Although we lost this game, our supporters must have had a clear glimpse of the sun after enduring so much depressing weather for so long.

It was obvious to all that if our club were fortunate enough to be able to sign more players of the calibre of St John, then real progress would be made in that long journey back to Division One.

With this international at Anfield, one major signing had been made, but I had another player under my observation who was my No. 2 target.

I had, in fact, been interested in him for a long time. He was a young player on the books of Dundee United who at that particular time was serving in the Army.

He was a giant of 6ft 2ins and nearly 15 stone in weight named Ronald Yeats.

Nothing was known of him in England, possibly because he was a part-time professional playing in Scottish Second Division football.

This part-time professional refers, of course, to has activities before his National Service, although

I suppose any player that is in the Service can be classed as part-time by reason of him spending so much time away from his club.

However, Yeats, prior to his Army service, lived and worked in Aberdeen and travelled roughly 60 miles to do his training and play home matches.

During his Army days, he was able to obtain sufficient passes to enable him to fly to Scotland every weekend to play for his club.

It was most important that he did this, because there is no doubt that at his feet lay a lot of the success which Dundee United were enjoying at the time. He did, in fact, lead them into Division One, winning the last match of the season in dramatic fashion to do so.

Persistence Pays Off

We made inquiries from the Dundee United club to the possibilities of securing Yeats' services but were told that there was no chance whatsoever of his coming to Liverpool.

However, from our own private sources of information, we knew that he felt his prospects of advancement in the game lay with crossing the

Position: *Centre-Half*
Birthplace: *Aberdeen*
Age: *23yrs 8mnths*
Height: *6ft 2ins*

Club Career

Dundee Utd: 1957 – present
Debut: *Jan 1, 1958*
v St Johnstone
League Appearances: *96*
League Goals: 1

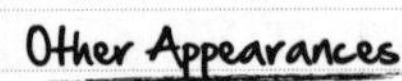

British Army
v Scotland U23
1960-61
Captain

Previous Clubs: *Aberdeen Lads Club.*

Other notes

** Worked as apprentice slaughterman before turning professional.*

** Currently doing National Service with Royal Army Service Corps.*

Expected fee = £22,000

border to England as so many of his illustrious predecessors in the football world have done before him.

We therefore persisted with our inquiries, but were met with definite refusals in the first place and then with the sort of figure which sounded more like the national debt than the transfer fee for a footballer. Everything said to us was with a note of discouragement.

Our telephone bill for calls to Dundee must, at this time, have been enormous, but I thought so much of Yeats not only as a good player at that time, but also as a player capable of development, that we had to persist.

Eventually our perseverance had its reward, or so we thought, because the chairman of Dundee United agreed to see two of our directors and me. We travelled north, the party consisting of Mr S.C. Reakes, Mr E. A. F. Sawyer and myself, but we were quite nonplussed by the Arctic reception we received.

We spent less than half-an-hour with the Dundee United chairman, who seemed quite unconcerned with the fact we had travelled several hundred miles to see him. The Liverpool party very quickly arrived at the same conclusion, which was that we were wasting our time at Dundee and that if there was one player who would never wear a red shirt in Liverpool, it was Yeats, so we returned to Anfield.

However, our information about Yeats wishing to come to England continued to be persistent that we really did not give up all hopes, even after the rebuff we had received.

We therefore kept in touch with this Scottish club and in the third week of July we had the pleasure of receiving the information that they were prepared to part with him and had put a price tag on him. They were, in point of fact, very unwilling to let him go as he was a key man in their set-up.

For my part, I saw Yeats as possibly another George Young of the future and certainly the man to weld our defence together in the way St John could weld the forwards.

We had received so many rebuffs to our earlier attempts to talk business that we found it difficult to believe that there was now a possibility of getting Yeats' services.

We left Anfield without delay, the party consisting of the chairman, the vice-chairman, Reuben Bennett and myself, and met the Dundee officials together with Ronnie Yeats in Edinburgh.

We had travelled by road all morning and

negotiations started immediately we arrived. The question of the transfer fee offered no difficulty and was agreed at once.

The snags which the talks disclosed were wages and agreeing a figure for the accrued share of benefit money. The former was comparatively easily settled, but the latter nearly put the negotiations on the rocks.

At one time it looked as though agreement could not be reached, but eventually a little goodwill by both sides enabled the matter to be settled and Ronnie Yeats signed for Liverpool on July 22, 1961.

We had such an anxious time in relation to Yeats since we first approached Dundee United about him that our success gave us the greatest elation.

This was our feeling and our immediate reaction was one of high spirits. I well remember Mr Reakes insisting on driving us non-stop to Liverpool; we did not even get a cup of tea on the way back!

*****

"The team selected as the senior side showed a few changes from the previous season, the major ones being Yeats at centre-half, White at full-back and, of course, the introduction of St John to lead the forwards."

My New Captain

Ronnie Yeats was with the Dundee United directors when we met them in Edinburgh, and to stand beside this giant after all the negotiations had been completed made me realise more than ever how commanding a figure he would be in the middle of the field, and very thankful he would be coming to Anfield and not any other club.

Prior to signing Yeats, I had seen Dick White and informed him of my intentions, because if negotiations went as we hoped, he would be deposed from the centre-half position by our new capture. It was my view that his great ability as a defensive player could better be used to our advantage transforming him into a right-back, a change of position which, from time to time immemorial, has taken place in the game, because the two positions go hand in glove.

A recent example of this is the case of Maurice Norman, of Tottenham, who started as a full-back and became a centre-half, and another is George Young, who commenced as a centre-half, changed to a full-back, a position he occupied for some years, after which he reverted to his former position.

I considered, then, that White could easily make this positional change, but I felt that it would be the right thing to acquaint him with my ideas even before any signing had taken place.

I should say now that Dick is one of the finest sportsmen in the game and was one of our best club men, and with this in mind, backed by the knowledge of his great experience, sterling character and influence over the younger players, I felt that he would make an ideal captain.

When I informed Dick of my decision, his reply was exactly what one would expect from such a character: "I'll do my best, boss."

Training had commenced a few days before signing Yeats and we were well underway with the first stage of the systematic programme which we had arranged.

Remember that this was July, and a very hot July into the bargain, and a great deal of credit is due to all the playing staff for the way they tackled the preliminary work prior to the start of the season.

Nothing that we asked the boys to do was too difficult and one could sense the feeling of optimism throughout the club.

Our next signing Yeats, however, was still in the Army, serving with the R.A.S.C and due to be 'demobbed' on Wednesday, August 16 from Yeovil, Somerset.

Although he had been on three weeks' leave, he found that the position of still being in the Army, but not of it, a bit unsettling and we therefore wanted to get him out of it without any delay.

Accordingly, I arranged for Tom Bush to drive down to Yeovil and bring Yeats back to the club immediately after his release routine had been completed.

I know that 'big Ronnie' (he is called that to distinguish him from Ronnie Moran) was a bit impressed with the sort of service Liverpool FC laid on for its players. He was more than a bit impressed when he was plunged into our training regime.

CURRENT SQUAD LIST FOR 1961/62 SEASON

Player	Position	Age
Bert Slater	Goalkeeper	25
Ron Yeats	Defender	23
Allan Jones	Defender	21
John Molyneux	Defender	30
Phil Ferns	Defender	23
Gerry Byrne	Defender	22
Ronnie Moran	Defender	27
Chris Lawler	Defender	17
Dick White	Defender	30
Ian Callaghan	Midfielder	19
Johnny Wheeler	Midfielder	33
Gordon Wallace	Midfielder	17
Jimmy Melia	Midfielder	23
Johnny Morrissey	Midfielder	21
Alan A'Court	Midfielder	26
Kevin Lewis	Midfielder	20
Gordon Milne	Midfielder	24
Tommy Leishman	Midfielder	23
Roger Hunt	Striker	23
Alf Arrowsmith	Striker	18
Ian St John	Striker	23
Willie Carlin	Striker	20

Average age = **23yrs**

Integrating The New Boys

Yeats had started later than the others because of his Army commitments and therefore we had to bring him along rather more quickly, so he must have wondered what he had been thrown into.

You must remember that this was his first experience of training as a full-time player and he found it far more severe than he had imagined and, at the same time, far more thorough.

He had been accustomed to doing almost nothing but track work, which, although it has its place in a training plan, is a most monotonous business.

He noticed at once the contrast when running is varied by spells of physical jerks and by far more ball play, such as five-a-side games, which help to sharpen a player's reactions.

What applied to Yeats also applied to Ian St John, but not quite to the same extent because Ian had been with us from the start of the training programme.

Both boys quickly realised that they had come to a club that which was in deadly earnest to succeed and I feel sure that, even though they were being trained harder than ever before in their lives, they both knew within themselves that this was a necessity.

Off the field, they had settled down well. They were fortunate to have Bert Slater and Tommy Leishman, both Scotsmen, in the club to show them around, and if Scotsmen cannot be friends, then I don't know who can.

Training went steadily on until we reached the time when we were ready to play the first practice match. The team selected as the senior side showed a few changes from the previous season, the major ones being Yeats at centre-half, White at full-back and, of course, the introduction of St John to lead the forwards.

The team read: Slater; White, Byrne; Milne, Yeats, Leishman; Lewis, Hunt, St John, Melia, A'Court. This I considered as my best combination to start the season.

Right from the start I was pleased with the way in which White settled into his new position: he added steadiness to the defence and in fact the whole team shaped very well in practice matches which have to be played so that we can safely say that players are, indeed, match fit.

Just prior to the public practice game on August 12, Yeats damaged the skin on one of his toes. It was nothing serious, but for some reason or the other, the wound turned septic.

MY STRONGEST XI
FOR SEASON AHEAD
St John
Centre-Forward
Hunt
Centre-Forward
Hickson
Centre-Forward
Lewis
Outside-Right
A'Court
Outside-Left
Melia
Inside-Forward
Leishman
Left-Half
Milne
Right-Half
White
Centre-Half
Byrne
Full-Back
Molyneux
Full-Back
Slater
Goalkeeper
Yeats
Centre-Half

Remember that he was still in the Army, not being due for release until the Wednesday following the public practice match and therefore still had to do a bit of travelling between Liverpool and his unit. The condition of his foot was causing a little anxiety. His own personal concern in the matter was whether the foot would prove too painful for him to do himself justice.

If you put yourself in his place, you will at once appreciate that he was on display for the first time to the hard core of our knowledgeable and critical supporters and the impression he created on them could well have a deep and lasting effect on his future.

He knew that he was less than 100 per cent fit and therefore unable to give of his best. When a player thinks along those lines, there is great hope for him and he rose in my estimation because of this outlook.

We talked the matter over and decided that we could best be guided by medical advice and accordingly Ronnie visited the club's doctor at 2pm on the day of the match. Although he was pronounced fit, he was still very apprehensive about playing, but a little persuasion got him on to the field.

There were about 8,500 enthusiasts who had come to see the new signings and their disappointment would have been considerable if the latest of them failed to appear. However, he played and although this was a practice match which nobody takes too seriously, there is no doubt that he created a very good impression on our ardent supporters and was, of course, delighted that he had played.

Ronnie returned to his unit for the last time after the practice match and returned as a civilian the following Wednesday. He thus missed a few days training just prior to the opening match of the season, but for the rest of the players, the last few days were hard ones and we thought that we had got them as fit as was humanely possible.

Preparing For Bristol Rovers

The coaching and playing staff, with the players, had spent a lot of time on tactical plans to suit the type of players we had and this, together with the great physical fitness of the lads, added up to a feeling of optimism tinged with caution.

I know everybody was looking forward to the start of the big effort which we were determined to make to win the prize which had been lost to us so often by such narrow margins.

My study of the fixture list gave me the impression that the early matches were difficult ones. I wanted a good start to the season for both practical and psychological reasons; in my estimation every point gained from the early games was worth far more to us that its actual face value, a point of view which I stressed to the team.

The first game was against Bristol Rovers in Bristol. On the Thursday before the game, I announced the team, which was identical to the senior side in the practice match, and on the Friday morning, we set off by coach.

Bristol is about 160 miles away and a difficult place to get to from Liverpool and more difficult place to leave for Liverpool if rail transport is used. Road transport enabled us to get back home on the Saturday night after the game and thus avoid Sunday travelling which is both slow and difficult.

Poor Yeats must have wondered about the logic of things when he found himself heading back to within 40 miles of the place he had left only two days previously.

1961/62 FIXTURE LIST

Division Two

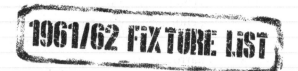

Date	Venue	Opposition	Date	Venue	Opposition
19.08.61	A	Bristol Rovers	16.12.61	H	Bristol Rovers
23.08.61	H	Sunderland	23.12.61	A	Leeds Utd
26.08.61	H	Leeds Utd	26.12.61	A	Rotherham Utd
30.08.61	A	Sunderland	30.12.62	H	Rotherham Utd
02.09.61	A	Norwich City	13.01.62	H	Norwich City
09.09.61	H	Scunthorpe Utd	20.01.62	A	Scunthorpe Utd
16.09.61	A	Brighton & H A	03.02.62	H	Brighton & HA
20.09.61	A	Newcastle Utd	07.02.62	A	Bury
23.09.61	H	Bury	24.02.62	H	Middlesbrough
30.09.61	A	Charlton Athletic	03.03.62	A	Walsall
04.10.61	H	Newcastle Utd	10.03.62	H	Derby County
07.10.61	A	Middlesbrough	17.03.62	A	Leyton Orient
14.10.61	H	Walsall	24.03.62	H	Preston NE
21.10.61	A	Derby County	31.03.62	A	Luton Town
28.10.61	H	Leyton Orient	07.04.62	H	Huddersfield Tn
04.11.61	A	Preston N E	14.04.62	A	Swansea Town
11.11.61	H	Luton Town	21.04.62	H	Southampton
18.11.61	A	Huddersfield Tn	23.04.62	H	Stoke City
25.11.61	H	Swansea Town	24.04.62	A	Stoke City
02.12.61	A	Southampton	28.04.62	A	Plymouth Argyle
09.12.61	H	Plymouth Argyle	30.04.62	H	Charlton Athletic

Introducing Gordon Milne

Readers may have noticed that mention of one important signing has been omitted, an omission which I am now rectifying. It took place towards the start of the 1960/61 season and I am therefore dealing with it out of sequence. The player in question is Gordon Milne.

Gordon is a young man who I have known for practically all his life as his father and I were colleagues and friends when we were playing for Preston North End, and during this period Gordon was born.

Gordon's father has one quality above others which I put first in my estimation of any man, and that is genuineness. This priceless attribute he has passed on to his son and in addition Gordon has inherited all his father's talent on the football field.

He has ability and courage and there is no doubt that he has benefitted to the greatest extent from the sage advice given to him by his father, based on the latter's great knowledge of the game.

I had been interested in Gordon for some time, but Johnny Wheeler was injured in the game against Middlesbrough in the latter part of the 1960/61 season and this unfortunate accident made it necessary to hasten the signing.

Accordingly, I visited Preston, on whose books Gordon was on at that time, and completed the transfer. Gordon's father was then trainer at Preston; had he been in a managerial capacity, I am not too sure that he would have been willing to part with his son.

He made his debut against Southampton and since then has been a regular and dependable member of the senior side.

* * * * *

"It appeared that we had arrived at a combination of players which could give a good account of itself in any company we would be likely to encounter."

Off To A Flyer

Bristol Rovers were our opponents for the opening game of the season which we all hoped would be the promotion one, and I know when I say that, I am speaking as much for all Liverpool supporters as anybody more intimately connected with the club.

That Saturday in August was a really hot one, much like a perfect afternoon for cricket rather than football and it was impossible to imagine the conditions of cold, mud and wet which footballers would have to endure later in the season.

We fielded what I considered to be our best combination of players, with Dick White as captain.

With the deplorable start we had made to the previous season (which as events showed, cost us promotion) in my memory, I regarded all the opening matches as vital ones and I had impressed this view on the team.

Always at the beginning of the season, there is a lot of nervous tension before a game and probably because of the knowledge of what a good start might mean, coupled with the fact that we had two new signings in a reconstituted team, which wanted to show itself off as a promotion possibility, the pre-match tension was far more emphatic than was normal.

Bristol Rovers had not a big reputation. They had a sprinkling of near-veterans in their team such as centre-forward Geoff Bradford (who had been one of the best in the game and who had, in the past, notched a hat-trick against us) and outside-left, Peter Hooper.

As in the case of many opening matches, the adjective 'great' could not be applied to this one. The theme for us was solidarity from back to front, with concentration on doing the simple things and not taking any chances. In this way, the first goal of the season came from Kevin Lewis, the only score in the first half.

SECOND DIVISION
19.08.1961
EASTVILLE STADIUM

Manager		Manager	
Bert Tann		Bill Shankly	
BRISTOL RVRS	 0	LIVERPOOL	 2

	Bristol Rvrs		Liverpool
1	Malcolm Norman	1	Bert Slater
2	Johnny Hills	2	Dick White
3	John Frowen	3	Gerry Byrne
4	Ray Mabbutt	4	Gordon Milne
5	Joe Davis	5	Ron Yeats
6	Brian Carter	6	Tommy Leishman
7	Harold Jarman	7	Kevin Lewis
8	Bobby Jones	8	Roger Hunt
9	Geoff Bradford	9	Ian St John
10	Ian Hamilton	10	Jimmy Melia
11	Peter Hooper	11	Alan A'Court

Referee:- H Horner
Attendance:- 19,438

Goals:- Lewis 7
Hills o/g 55

In the second half, the boys settled down and played sound, methodical football which resulted in a goal from Jimmy Melia (although this was subsequently credited as being a John Hills own goal). After this we might have scored on numerous occasions, but some good goalkeeping left the final score at two-nil.

To me, the overall performance was quite a solid one and I was content with this modest win over a side which was eventually to finish at exactly the opposite end of the table to us.

Both Ian St John and Ronnie Yeats came out of the game with credit. Of the two, Ronnie was the less experienced player and confessed to feeling like a jelly immediately before the match.

He had found the tempo of the game faster than he had anticipated and said that it took him all of the first half to get accustomed to the extra speed at which it was played.

However, I was more than satisfied with their form, taken as a whole and considering that this was their first league match.

The return journey found the party in a spirit of jubilation and optimism. For my part, I am a cautious man, but I felt that the changes which had been made had already justified themselves.

Dick White had quickly settled down in his new position and gave the impression that he had occupied it for years. His presence gave an appearance of solidarity to the defence with each man playing his part and in spells linking up with the forward line.

With St John leading the forwards, the attack, I thought, would give a lot of trouble to defences in the weeks ahead. And with this feeling of satisfaction, we returned home, having taken the first successful step along what we hoped would be the road to the first division.

On the same day at Anfield, the Reserves had beaten Stoke Reserves 2-0. This win was marred by an unfortunate accident to Gordon Wallace, who fractured a leg, an accident which was to keep him out of the game for practically the remainder of the season.

On the Monday morning, we gathered at Melwood for our training session, after which we discussed the Bristol Rovers game in detail and formulated our plans for the match against Sunderland which was to take place on the next Wednesday evening, a game which I considered to be one of the most vital of the season.

Outstanding At Anfield

Sunderland would be fielding players such as Charlie Hurley, Stan Anderson, Brian Clough and Harry Hooper, and a team such as this, coupled with the fact that St John and Yeats were due to make their home debut, would be liable to create an atmosphere which could make Anfield bubble over.

The game was played before a crowd of nearly 40,000, most of them our own supporters and the book shows that we won 3-0.

However, what must have given the greatest satisfaction to our fans was not the margin of this victory, but the manner in which it was gained and the way our players stood up to this tremendous test. The method of play and the general bearing of the team must have impressed everyone.

It was unfortunate that Hurley cut his head and in consequence had to play in the forward line in the second half, but in spite of this, Sunderland contributed a lot towards the entertainment by a fine display of football.

As a matter of fact, during the interval, I learned that Hurley was expected to do well in the forwards as this was by no means the first time he had played in the front line, and they were even so optimistic as to expect that he would pull the game out of the fire for them.

Roger Hunt opened the scoring with what was to be the first of his record-breaking series of goals and the teams changed ends with this as the only score.

In the second half, Kevin Lewis made the score 2-0 with a goal which the Kop will remember for a very long time; he fairly slashed the ball into the roof of the net.

The scoring was completed by Hunt and these three goals confirmed the view which I had formed after the Bristol game, that our forwards would prove capable of reaching great heights, not only as entertainers, but in the equally important role of goal-getters.

Kevin Lewis is likely to strike at any time, Alan A'Court working like a beaver and the inside men, Hunt and Melia, linking with St John as though they had played together for years, it would be a very soured critic who would disagree with this view.

My notes on this match show that everyone played his part in an outstanding game and given freedom from injury, it appeared that we had

SECOND DIVISION
23.08.1961
ANFIELD

Manager			Manager	
Bill Shankly			Alan Brown	
LIVERPOOL	3 		SUNDERLAND	0 
1	Bert Slater		1	Peter Wakeham
2	Dick White		2	Colin Nelson
3	Gerry Byrne		3	Len Ashurst
4	Gordon Milne		4	Stan Anderson
5	Ron Yeats		5	Charlie Hurley
6	Tommy Leishman		6	Jimmy McNab
7	Kevin Lewis		7	Harry Hooper
8	Roger Hunt		8	George Herd
9	Ian St John		9	Brian Clough
10	Jimmy Melia		10	Willie McPheat
11	Alan A'Court		11	Jack Overfield

Goals:- Hunt 48, 83
Lewis 78

Attendance:- 48,900
Referee:- W Clements

arrived at a combination of players which could give a good account of itself in any company we would be likely to encounter.

The success of St John and Yeats must have put great heart into our supporters. I was, as you can imagine, desperately anxious for them to do well in this, their first home game, not only for the result of this particular match, but for the impression which they would make on the crowd, for this first impression could have a lasting effect upon their future.

I shall never forget the first time Yeats touched the ball. It had been slung up the field, high between him and Clough, and Ronnie rose to it like the giant he is, giving Clough no chance whatsoever. The reaction of the crowd was such that one was left with no doubt that here was a character who would quickly establish himself as one of the favourites.

His play throughout gave the impression that we had a man who would become a sheet anchor for Liverpool for many seasons to come.

As for St John, our supporters had previously had a view of him in the game against Everton at the end of the previous season when he had treated them to a hat-trick.

Against Sunderland, he failed to score but apart from that, the way he led the line was brilliant. He caused the Sunderland defence a heap of trouble and confirmed the good impression which he had given at Goodison.

Know Your Enemy

We had thus played two, won two, with five goals for and none against. Of the two scalps dangling from our belt, one was from a team which was generally regarded as being among the favourites for promotion and therefore, if my earlier assessment of the value of the points from games at the beginning of the season is correct, surely this particular win was worth double the two points we had gained if only from the view of the team's morale. I thought so, anyway.

Our second step had been made along the difficult road which we had to travel and although the team had done everything which had been asked of it, my knowledge of football tempered my optimism with caution.

In this early part of the season, there are fixtures being played every night somewhere in England

LEAGUE STANDINGS AUG 23RD 1961...

	Team	P	W	D	L	F	A	Pts	GA
1	Liverpool	2	2	0	0	5	0	4	0.00
2	Leeds United	2	2	0	0	4	1	4	4.00
3	Derby County	2	2	0	0	6	3	4	2.00
4	Huddersfield Tn	2	1	1	0	6	2	3	3.00
5	Norwich City	2	1	1	0	5	3	3	1.67
6	Newcastle United	2	1	1	0	1	0	3	0.00
7	Rotherham United	1	1	0	0	2	1	2	2.00
8	Luton Town	2	1	0	1	4	3	2	1.33
9	Southampton	2	1	0	1	4	3	2	1.33
10	Scunthorpe Utd	2	0	2	0	5	5	2	1.00
11	Walsall	2	1	0	1	4	4	2	1.00
12	Bury	2	1	0	1	3	3	2	1.00
13	Swansea Town	2	0	2	0	2	2	2	1.00
14	Plymouth Argyle	2	1	0	1	3	6	2	0.50
15	Stoke City	2	0	1	1	3	4	1	0.75
16	Brighton & HA	2	0	1	1	4	6	1	0.67
17	Charlton Athletic	2	0	1	1	2	3	1	0.67
18	Preston North End	2	0	1	1	2	5	1	0.40
19	Leyton Orient	2	0	1	1	1	3	1	0.33
20	Middlesbrough	1	0	0	1	3	4	0	0.75
21	Sunderland	2	0	0	2	3	7	0	0.43
22	Bristol Rovers	2	0	0	2	0	4	0	0.00

and many of these concerned clubs which we would meet during the season.

It was my policy to see these games with a view to assessing the strengths (and weaknesses) of these sides. Even if a team has no particular strong or weak point, many of them play to a pattern which can easily be detected and the advantage of knowing this pattern beforehand, to me, is obvious.

However, there is more than one school of thought on this subject but the one to which I subscribe is know your enemy and in order to do this I suppose that I must have travelled many thousands of miles during the season.

I did, in fact, manage to watch nearly every team in the Second Division before we played them.

A case in point occurred very shortly after our game against Sunderland when I went to Preston to see their match against Swansea, to me a valuable trip because we were due to meet both these teams before the end of November.

Apart from seeing these Second Division matches, I added to my total number of miles travelled by going to see various players in whom we might be interested and by several visits to see one particular man whom I thought was ideal to strengthen another position with which I was not 100 per cent satisfied.

*****

"It was a bright sunny evening and this fact presented a tactical problem. I made inquiries from the locals about the time it took for the sun to fall below the top of the stand. I even tried timing its rate of settling, but this turned out to be quite futile."

Our Most Exuberant Mood

Following our win against Sunderland the players had a rest day. This period of the year was probably hotter than any time during mid-summer and during conditions such as this, a short rest after the exertions of a game can do far more for a team than a continuance of training; indeed, without a break there would certainly be harmful effects.

On the Saturday, we were due to play Leeds United at Anfield and the day prior to this we met at Melwood for training and to discuss in detail the games played and in particular the one against Sunderland.

There was no doubt in my mind that, although the game had been played at home, our win had struck a decisive early blow at a team which many good judges considered likely to take Second Division honours.

More than this, the solid win had imparted a feeling of confidence to the boys and it was part of my tack to uphold this but to take care that it did not become complacency.

We regarded Leeds as a good side. They had started the season on the same winning note as ourselves having beaten Brighton away and Charlton at home and I knew that Don Revie had high hopes of making a good show in the promotion race.

However, they ran into a bad storm at Anfield, striking our boys in their most exuberant mood. Until half-time they gave a good account of themselves, but under the humid conditions in which the match was played, they wilted in the second half, losing 5-0.

In the Leeds side was William Bremner, a player of great ability and courage, who would give a good account of himself in any company, but even his tireless efforts could do nothing to reduce the margin of defeat.

So the boys came off the pitch with the record of having won the first three games, scoring 10 times and conceding none. What better start could we have to a season?

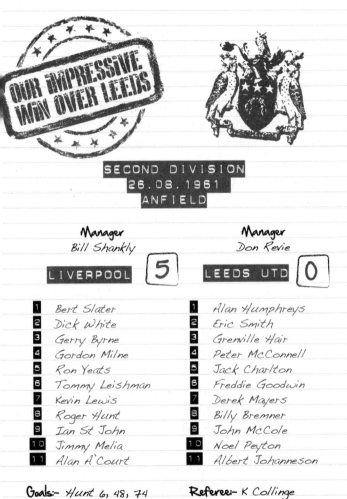

SECOND DIVISION
26.08.1961
ANFIELD

Manager		Manager	
Bill Shankly		Don Revie	
LIVERPOOL	5	LEEDS UTD	0

	Liverpool		Leeds Utd
1	Bert Slater	1	Alan Humphreys
2	Dick White	2	Eric Smith
3	Gerry Byrne	3	Grenville Hair
4	Gordon Milne	4	Peter McConnell
5	Ron Yeats	5	Jack Charlton
6	Tommy Leishman	6	Freddie Goodwin
7	Kevin Lewis	7	Derek Mayers
8	Roger Hunt	8	Billy Bremner
9	Ian St John	9	John McCole
10	Jimmy Melia	10	Noel Peyton
11	Alan A'Court	11	Albert Johanneson

Goals:- Hunt 6, 48, 74
Lewis 53 pen
Melia 68

Referee:- K Collinge
Attendance:- 42,950

I Even Tried Timing The Sun

A study of the fixture list had shown that we had an opportunity, by winning our early games, of doing a lot of damage to serious rivals in the matter of promotion. As indicated earlier, Sunderland was one of the clubs and we were due to meet them at Roker Park on the following Wednesday.

Owing to Sunderland being one of our more remote fixtures, we had to decide whether to travel on the Tuesday afternoon, stay overnight and kick our heels for the whole of the Wednesday until the early evening kick-off, or catch the morning train on the day of the match which would get us to our destination at 2pm.

The former plan was not considered a very good one and accordingly a light-hearted but very determined party caught the morning train on the day of the match.

After food in the afternoon, the players went to bed for a couple of hours and then travelled to Roker Park in time for them to have a shower before the game. We could not afford for any of them going on to the field not properly awake after his afternoon nap.

Immediately on arrival at the ground, the players inspected the pitch. This was well before the time for the start, but the ground was beginning to fill and one could sense an atmosphere building up similar to that at Anfield the previous week.

It was a bright sunny evening and this fact presented a tactical problem which I found difficult to solve; in fact I never solved it.

The sun was commencing to set behind one of the goals and it was obvious that until it dipped below the levels of the stand, defenders would find it almost impossible to 'find' a ball against a background of blinding light.

I made inquiries from the locals about the time it took for the sun to fall below the top of the stand, but I was not able to get any information. I even tried timing its rate of settling, but this turned out to be quite futile.

After all this, Dick White lost the toss and I could scarcely believe my eyes when I saw that Sunderland had chosen to play into the sun.

I had known that, just as we at Anfield like to defend the Kop goal in the first half, so they had a favourite goal to defend when they won the toss, but it scarcely seemed credible to me that they would go to the lengths of playing against the sun in order to satisfy preference.

When the teams lined up, I had the feeling that this was a genuine test of strength, for although we had a convincing win against Sunderland at Anfield, playing this team on their own pitch was a different proposition entirely and the outcome of the game would give us some idea of what we could expect in future matches.

Both sides played brilliantly in the first half and even before Hunt opened the score, we had created five good chances, none of which produced goals.

However, Roger's effort was quickly followed by another from Ian St John's head, but although we were winning by two clear goals until almost half-time, I thought that we had very little good luck, a statement borne out by a goal against us credited to Clough but which actually touched Yeats, thus deflecting the ball past Slater.

This was only seconds before half-time, so we changed over with a 2-1 lead. In my opinion, conceding a goal so close to the half-time whistle is a sore blow, but in this case I felt that we had the edge on Sunderland, particularly as I knew how fit the boys were.

In consequence, I was able to tell the team with all sincerity: "Well played; forget that goal against you and enjoy your game in the second half."

SECOND DIVISION
30.08.1961
ROKER PARK

Manager Alan Brown		Manager Bill Shankly	
SUNDERLAND	 1	LIVERPOOL	 4
1	Peter Wakeham	1	Bert Slater
2	Colin Nelson	2	Dick White
3	Len Ashurst	3	Gerry Byrne
4	Stan Anderson	4	Gordon Milne
5	Dickie Rooks	5	Ron Yeats
6	Jimmy McNab	6	Tommy Leishman
7	Harry Hooper	7	Kevin Lewis
8	Amby Fogarty	8	Roger Hunt
9	Brian Clough	9	Ian St John
10	Willie McPheat	10	Jimmy Melia
11	Jack Overfield	11	Alan A'Court

Goal:- Clough 45

Goals:- Hunt 26, 69
St John 39, 90

Attendance:- 47,261

This they did and I think that they played even better in the second half than the first. Both Hunt and St John scored again without reply and thus emphasised our superiority over Sunderland both home and away.

Everyone Played Their Part

In a game in which everyone played his part well, one hesitates to make comments other than to pay tribute to the side as a whole. However, my summing up of the team at this point showed that Bert Slater had had a very easy passage; Dick White was as steady and sure as expected; Gerry Byrne was playing well and gaining experience, and although a quiet fellow, he was full of determination on the field.

Gordon Milne was playing flawless football and our big boys, Ronnie Yeats was playing like the giant he is, Tommy Leishman had settled down and, having mellowed in his game, was playing extremely well.

Coming to the forwards, at this early stage, Kevin Lewis had showed that he had not lost

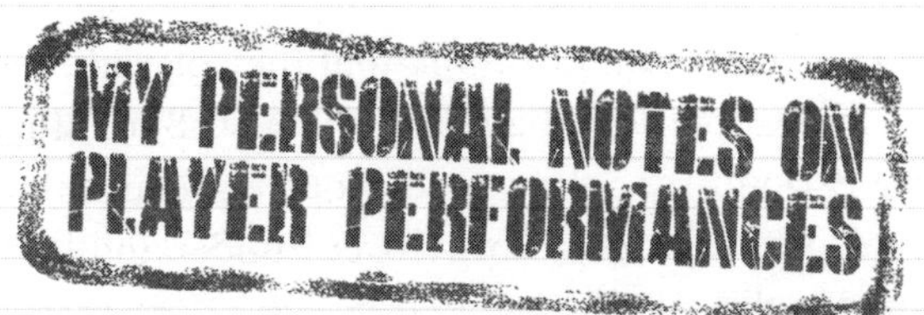

Early season summary

Player	Comments
Bert Slater	Rarely troubled, very easy passage
Dick White	Steady and reliable as ever
Gerry Byrne	Playing well; gaining experience; quiet but determined
Gordon Milne	Flawless
Ronnie Yeats	Performing like a giant
Tommy Leishman	Mellowing, playing extremely well
Kevin Lewis	Outstanding shooting power
Roger Hunt	Overcome injury, hard worker, great goalscorer
Ian St John	Working hard and knitting front line together
Jimmy Melia	Flying start to season; stand-out display v Sunderland
Alan A'Court	Practical joker; another key player at Roker Park

his goalscoring ability and his shooting power had been an outstanding feature of the games played.

It was obvious, too, Roger Hunt had fully recovered from the injury which he has sustained when playing against Nantes, was working hard and what is more, was finding the net with the ball.

His understanding with St John and Melia was complete enough to satisfy one even as critical as myself and augured well for the future.

St John had scored only twice, but was knitting the forwards together by his hard work, by fetching and carrying and plying his colleagues with the ball.

Jimmy Melia had started the season in a wonderful fashion and his display at Roker was probably the best of his career to date.

Jovial Alan A'Court (who is worth his weight in gold in the dressing room with his practical jokes) was quite on a par with Jimmy Melia at Roker, which is high praise indeed.

If one had to pin-point the highlight of the game at Roker Park, unquestionably it would be St John's first league goals and one shuddered to think what the noise would've been like at Anfield had they been scored there.

A Bonus For The Boys

In retrospect, it is interesting to reflect that Roger Hunt has already brought his tally to seven in the four matches played, but at that time nobody could have visualised that he would retain his shooting form so well that he would finish the season with over 40 league goals to his credit.

As you may imagine, the jubilation of the boys knew no bounds in the dressing room after the match. We had time to feel a bit sorry for Sunderland as Hurley was still unfit and unable to play, but against this was the undeniable fact that St John's performance would have taxed the best centre-half in the game.

Even if Hurley had been playing, I do not think that it could have changed the result and so we had the great satisfaction of having the points in the bag and at the same time having given the paying customers real value for their money.

We stayed overnight in Sunderland and during the evening I was in conversation with some of the very knowledgeable Wearside football followers (and some from Tyneside too) and was more than interested to find that their talking point was the fitness of the Liverpool team and just how such fitness can be achieved so early in the season.

It gave me the greatest satisfaction to hear some comments; I should have been less than human if this were not the case.

The Press gave the game a good write-up the following day, which means a lot to any team, particularly when even the most modest of them felt that it is deserved.

As far as the players were concerned, this win was just what they wanted because although before it, they had done everything asked of them in the way of training, from now on fitness became a matter of dedication.

About this period, the board had been considering the players' remuneration and they had decided that if the performance of the boys were such that good gates resulted, then it would be justice for the team to participate in the extra revenue.

Accordingly, appreciation of their efforts was made by putting them on an attendance bonus, which was a much more practical method than any other; a vote of thanks, for instance!

The Friday following the Sunderland game found us once more at Melwood preparing for another vital match against Norwich on the following day, so that we had another long trip to anticipate.

There was a saying among the players at this time that you had to be fit in order to survive the travelling.

*****

"The coach which should have conveyed to us to the station failed to arrive. Telephone calls got no result; the Norwich officials were unable to get taxis for us and the only transport available was the Norwich goalkeeper's car."

Marooned In Colchester On My Birthday

The first month of the season gave us five away matches and three at home. Those played away from Anfield (Bristol Rovers, Sunderland, Norwich, Brighton and Newcastle) involved something like 1,800 miles of travelling, which, because of the heatwave which had greeted the start of the football season, proved more than a bit irksome.

It seemed that no sooner had we arrived from Sunderland, than we were on the move for Norwich. Those of my readers who happened to be in the Services during the war and stationed in East Anglia will know what difficulty there can be in making the journey to and from Liverpool.

With a football team, the problem is to make the journey and, at the same time, arrive fresh for the game. Hotel accommodation in East Anglia is difficult and we had been unable to find a suitable place to stay in the Norwich area on the Friday night.

We were left with no alternative to travel to London on Friday afternoon, spend the night at the hotel which we always use when playing in the London area, and catch a train from Liverpool Street on Saturday morning.

This was the plan and it worked out well in as much as we had a restful night and caught a train for Norwich at about 10am.

This was on September 2, which happened to be my birthday, a fact which leaked out and made me the subject of a good deal of ribbing from the boys. They did, however, promise me a couple of points as a present.

The programme which we had so carefully made came to an abrupt halt when the train did the same thing somewhere in the middle of a lovely bit of country approximately in the Colchester area.

Forty minutes later it was still stationary and we were marooned there with no means of communication with anybody and visions of not arriving in time to complete our fixture.

This particular day was one of the hottest of the year and the discomfort of the heat in the train, which was reminiscent of the atmosphere in a Turkish bath, did nothing to help our peace of mind.

However, we eventually arrived at Norwich with just half-an-hour to spare before the kick-off. The ground presented an astonishing sight of the large crowd of men in shirt sleeves and women in summer dresses. It looked more like a crowd watching a cricket match.

Heat In The Hay Field

The pitch is an extremely small one and the long grass on it at the time was burnt brown and gave the impression of a hay field which had remained uncut, and the turf under it was dry and bone-hard.

The players had been very patient during our hold-up, but it probably had an unsettling effect on them, so they took a little time to settle down.

However, once they did, the game came well up to expectations and even the conditions under which it was played did not prevent a marvellous exhibition of football. How both sides stuck the pace when spectators were gasping for breath in the heat was quite amazing.

Norwich struck the first blow, for following a short corner in an attempt to intercept a shot, Yeats deflected the ball past Slater with the inside of his thigh.

During the interval, there was more thirst-quenching than I can remember in any game, the players seeming to be quite dehydrated and drinking copious supplies of orange juice to quench their awful thirsts.

You can judge what it was like when I tell you that Barry Butler, the Norwich centre-half, lost 6lbs during the game.

The second half was when team spirit, fighting spirit and fitness really told. Most of the players pulled down their stockings in an attempt to keep a little cooler.

Kevin Lewis was one of those and he must have sensed that his opposite number, Ashman (who is not in the first flush of youth as footballers go) was feeling the pace and Kevin was thus able to carry the ball and fairly blast his shots at goal.

About ten minutes after half-time, one of those hit Roger Hunt's leg and was diverted into the goal

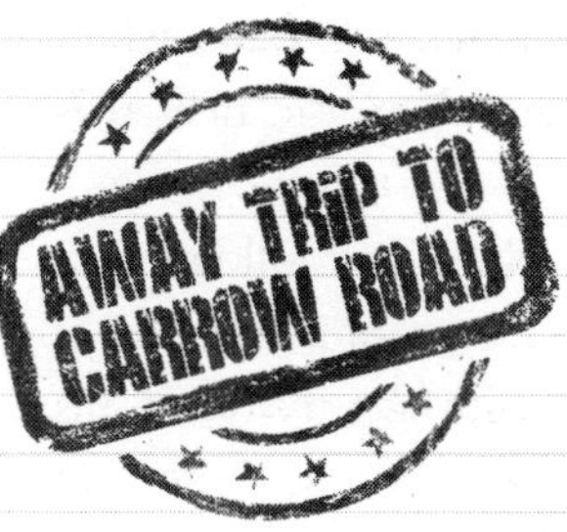

SECOND DIVISION
02.09.1961
CARROW ROAD

Manager Archibald Macaulay		**Manager** Bill Shankly	
NORWICH CITY	1	LIVERPOOL	2
1	Sandy Kennon	1	Bert Slater
2	Bryan Thurlow	2	Dick White
3	Ron Ashman	3	Gerry Byrne
4	Roy McCrohan	4	Gordon Milne
5	Barry Butler	5	Ron Yeats
6	Matt Crowe	6	Tommy Leishman
7	Gerry Mannion	7	Kevin Lewis
8	Terry Allcock	8	Roger Hunt
9	Jimmy Conway	9	Ian St John
10	Bunny Larkin	10	Jimmy Melia
11	George Waites	11	Alan A'Court

Goal:- Yeats o/g

Goals:- Hunt 63, 86

Attendance:- 28,049

for the equaliser. Just as this was a blow to Norwich, so it was a tonic to us. We really turned on the heat, playing wonderful football, with the forwards causing the Norwich defence lots of trouble.

About ten minutes from the end, St John flicked a ball through the middle for Hunt to chase. He picked it up, carried it for a distance although embarrassed by three Norwich men and then fairly lashed it into the net to the great delight of our players.

The referee signalled a goal, but then consulted his linesman and promptly disallowed it for some obscure reason. This was a real blow, but far from discouraging the team, it seemed to act as a spur and shortly before the final whistle, Hunt stabbed the winner over the goalkeeper's head.

In this way I got my birthday present and was very thankful for it. Things had not been going exactly according to plan in the morning, but there is no doubt they finished well to the delight of everybody concerned.

The Norwich Keeper's Car

That was my immediate reaction to the result, but we were due for a further setback on this memorable day.

The coach which should have conveyed to us to the station failed to arrive. Telephone calls got no result; the Norwich officials were unable to get taxis for us and the only transport available was the Norwich goalkeeper's car.

Sandy Kennon very decently took as many of the party as he could pile in, a kindness for which we were very grateful, and those less lucky were left to pick up their bags and, with the temperatures in the '80s, enjoy a brisk mile-and-a-half walk to the station. We caught the train with nothing to spare.

However, such was the elation of the party that if someone had told us that we had to walk to London, there would have been very few long faces, if any.

That was the end of our troubles. We caught the midnight train, on which sleepers had been booked, to Liverpool where we were met by a coach which enabled us to arrive home in the early hours of the morning.

Although the season had been in progress for such a short time, it had been an extremely strenuous one.

We had played five games in fifteen days and travelled over a thousand miles to do so, and we were glad to be able to contemplate the immediate future with no midweek matches.

This would enable us to revert to the normal

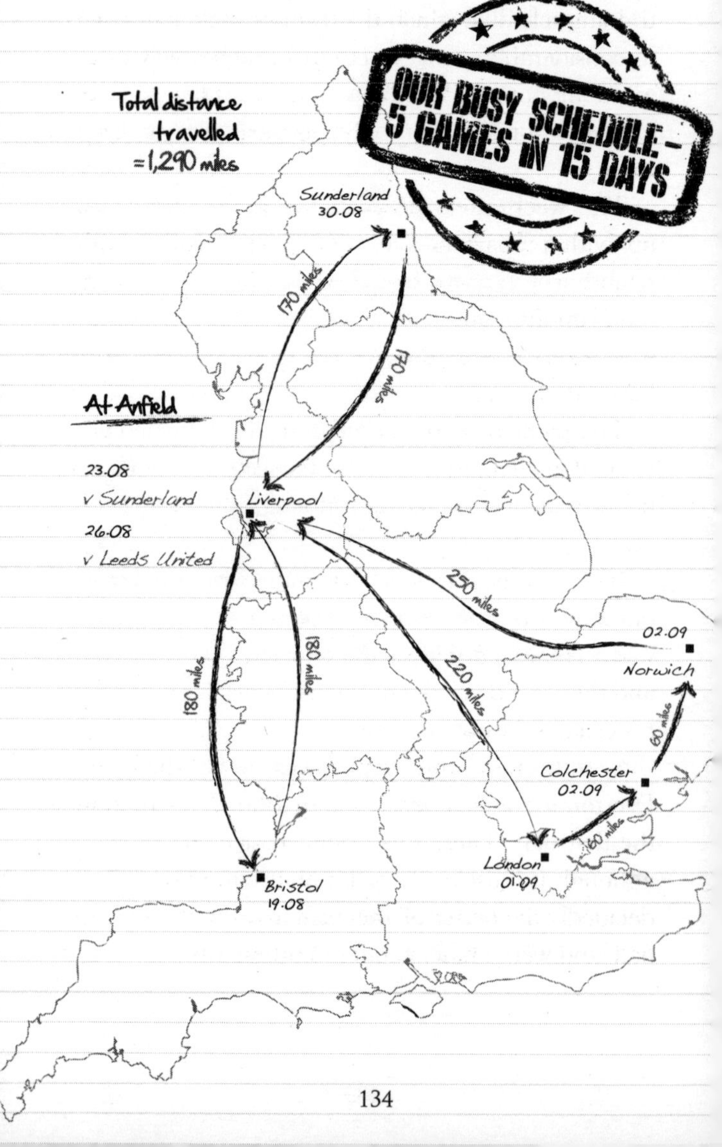
OUR BUSY SCHEDULE –
5 GAMES IN 15 DAYS
Total distance
travelled
=1,290 miles
At Anfield
23.08
v Sunderland
26.08
v Leeds United
Sunderland
30.08
170 miles
170 miles
Liverpool
250 miles
02.09
Norwich
220 miles
180 miles
180 miles
60 miles
Colchester
02.09
60 miles
London
01.09
Bristol
19.08

training schedule which the training staff had been to considerable pains to set out in such a way as to avoid monotony. We knew that the players were extremely fit and our only problem was to keep them so.

The week after the Norwich game was taken up with preparations for our home fixture with Scunthorpe. Nobody would ever see this team among the glamour clubs of football, but nevertheless they were a very useful side which we had always found a hard nut to crack.

This game proved no exception. They turned out to be dour fighters who were extremely anxious to be the first club to take our unbeaten tag away from us.

In the early stages, we created many openings, but only two goals resulted. The first of these came when Hemstead deflected a shot into his own goal and the second was from Alan A'Court, a reward for his usual industrious game.

Scunthorpe's only reply was from their ex-Everton inside forward Godfrey, who also scored in the first half. These three goals ended the scoring, although it must be recorded that Scunthorpe had decidedly the better of the exchanges in the second half and were unlucky to lose both points.

SECOND DIVISION
09.09.1961
ANFIELD

Manager	Manager
Bill Shankly	Richard Duckworth

LIVERPOOL  2

SCUNTHORPE  1

	Liverpool		Scunthorpe
1	Bert Slater	1	Joe Turner
2	Dick White	2	Derek Hemstead
3	Gerry Byrne	3	Jack Brownsword
4	Gordon Milne	4	Archie Gibson
5	Ron Yeats	5	Barry Horstead
6	Tommy Leishman	6	Ron Howells
7	Kevin Lewis	7	Jack Marriott
8	Roger Hunt	8	Brian Godfrey
9	Ian St John	9	Barrie Thomas
10	Jimmy Melia	10	Joe Bonson
11	Alan A'Court	11	Arthur Thorpe

Goals:- Hemstead o/g 12
A'Court 23

Goal:- Godfrey

Attendance:- 46,837

However, we were most thankful to maintain our 100 per cent record. I had been told by one of the Scunthorpe officials before the game that they fully expected to beat us, mainly on the grounds that 'you have had a good run which can't last; you must be beaten some time'.

What he said was true, of course, but personally I should have required a much sounder reason than this for such optimism.

First Point Dropped

For the match the following week we had to make another long trip, this time Brighton. We travelled there the day preceding the match, still in the heatwave which was giving holidaymakers the tan of a lifetime, but which was beginning to be a bit of a bore to footballers.

Brighton's ground is a small, compact one and a capacity gate of about 19,000 in shirt sleeve order saw the team on a day which was even hotter than the day on which we met Norwich.

We had a really hard fight, but the winning goal would not come; on the other hand our defence did not let us down so that although we failed to win our

SECOND DIVISION
16.09.1961
GOLDSTONE GROUND

Manager		Manager	
George Curtis		Bill Shankly	
BRIGHTON & H.A		LIVERPOOL	

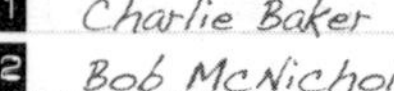

	Brighton & H.A		Liverpool
1	Charlie Baker	1	Bert Slater
2	Bob McNichol	2	Dick White
3	Dave Smith	3	Gerry Byrne
4	Jack Bertolini	4	Gordon Milne
5	Roy Jennings	5	Ron Yeats
6	Steve Burtenshaw	6	Tommy Leishman
7	Mike Tiddy	7	Kevin Lewis
8	Ian McNeill	8	Roger Hunt
9	Tony Nicholas	9	Ian St John
10	Johnny Goodchild	10	Jimmy Melia
11	Bobby Laverick	11	Alan A'Court

Attendance:- 18,764

seventh match on the run, we were still unbeaten.

My own feeling was that we had lost a record but I was thankful that we had not lost the game.

Losing the 100 per cent tag in this fashion was more than worth the loss of one point, because carrying a label of this sort was beginning to become a source of worry for the players, with the result that they suffered from more nervous tension before a game than some members of teams with less enviable records.

Without this tension, I hoped that they would be able to settle down more quickly on the field and get on with the job of winning their matches.

We returned home the same night, a party well content with the way things had gone, and left the train at Crewe where we had arranged for a coach to meet us, which enabled us to arrive home in the early hours of the morning.

This was considered far preferable to travelling on Sunday, particularly as we were due to resume midweek travelling again with our away fixture against Newcastle the following Wednesday.

*****

"It seemed to me that our success had inoculated even the lukewarm supporter and turned him into a regular fan."

Silencing Geordie Bravado

After losing our 100% record at Brighton, the tension was somewhat lessened, but it was still greater than if we had lost at Brighton. Every team we played had everything to gain and nothing to lose.

With this thought always in our minds, we prepared to play a match which I considered as vital to us as those against Sunderland. This was against Newcastle at St James' Park, a club steeped in tradition as prior to the war, Tyneside was recognised as a home and nursery of English football.

Very few clubs existed which did not have one or more North Easterners on their books. Such names as Raich Carter, Ronnie Starling, Warney Creswell, Sam Bartram, Jackie Milburn and our own Albert Stubbins, to name a few, spring easily to mind.

As in our case, Newcastle were wallowing unhappily in the Second Division and were finding it difficult to extricate themselves as we were. For a side with such a long history of greatness behind them, it is one of football's tragedies.

We adopted the same routine for this game as the one in Sunderland, travelling on the morning on the train to Newcastle, having a meal on arrival and insisting the players have a rest before the match.

We found the atmosphere in this city of football very tense which could be traced to the record of the Liverpool club and emphasised by a statement by one of the Newcastle officials to the effect that Newcastle would beat us on the bone-hard pitch. To me this savoured more bravado than confidence.

The team set about playing the most composed and methodical football which they had yet produced (and that is the highest praise I can give them), creating chance after chance and were unfortunate not to have run up a big score early in the game.

Even Kevin Lewis had a penalty saved, but we must give credit to Hollins, as to any keeper who saves a penalty. Indeed, Newcastle owe a debt of gratitude to their keeper for his wonderful game and it was due in no small measure to his efforts that the score was kept as low as it ultimately turned out to be.

In complete contrast to our short, methodical game, Newcastle's plan turned out to be a series of long, high kicks down the middle, tactics which were greatly to the liking of Ronnie Yeats and our defenders in general.

An own goal from Heslop and one from Gordon Milne completed our scoring, although with the game at 2-0, Lewis had the penalty saved.

Hale replied for Newcastle, which turned out to be the final score, so that to the great delight of all the boys and, indeed, to that of everyone connected with the club, we were still unbeaten, had played five matches away and had collected 15 out of a possible 16 points with a goal average showing 20 for and only four against.

This was a very satisfactory state of affairs and almost as important, we had no injuries to contend with and consequently had not found it necessary to make any team changes.

SECOND DIVISION
20.09.1961
ST JAMES' PARK

Manager			Manager	
Charles Mitten			Bill Shankly	
NEWCASTLE UTD			LIVERPOOL	
1	Dave Hollins		1	Bert Slater
2	Dick Keith		2	Dick White
3	Alf McMichael		3	Gerry Byrne
4	Jackie Bell		4	Gordon Milne
5	George Heslop		5	Ron Yeats
6	George Dalton		6	Tommy Leishman
7	Len White		7	Kevin Lewis
8	Ivor Allchurch		8	Roger Hunt
9	Ken Hale		9	Ian St John
10	Ken Leek		10	Jimmy Melia
11	Liam Tuohy		11	Alan A'Court

Goals:- Hale
Attendance:- 38,180

Goals:- Milne 10
Heslop o/g 43

I could not help but feel that the gods were smiling upon us at this stage, and this made me more than ever determined to do everything in my power to get every possible point in case we were forced to make changes which might bring to an end our winning vein.

The next opposition was Bury at Anfield, not one of the glamour clubs of football, but the way which we were playing and the results which we were achieving attracted a gate of 47,000, then the largest of the season.

It seemed to me that our success had inoculated even the lukewarm supporter and turned him into a regular fan.

A crowd like that is a great stimulus for a team and the boys were determined to show what they could do. Inside the first minute, Melia opened the scoring, but even while the movement leading to the score was still in progress, Turner, the Bury right-half, was lying on the ground, injured.

He had to leave the field and did not return, a crippling blow to our Lancashire friends, and it put them in an impossible position as far as even making a game of it.

They lost 5-0 and we must give all credit to their ten men for the fight which they made, but

SECOND DIVISION
23.09.1961
ANFIELD

Manager			Manager	
Bill Shankly			David Russell	
LIVERPOOL	5		BURY	 0
1	Bert Slater		1	Frank Adams
2	Dick White		2	Brian Gallagher
3	Gerry Byrne		3	Bobby Conroy
4	Gordon Milne		4	Brian Turner
5	Ron Yeats		5	Bob Stokoe
6	Tommy Leishman		6	Gordon Atherton
7	Kevin Lewis		7	Bill Holden
8	Roger Hunt		8	Frank Beaumont
9	Ian St John		9	Don Watson
10	Jimmy Melia		10	Alan Jackson
11	Alan A'Court		11	Johnny Hubbard

Goals:- Melia 1, 46
St John 7
Hunt 64
Lewis 70

Attendance:- 46, 609

although the loss of Turner may have affected the margin of our win, it is difficult to visualise any other result with the team in such a rampant mood. So the triumphant march continued and the football world was beginning to take notice of our progress.

Accused Of Taking The Mickey

At the start of the season we had played five games in the first fifteen days and after a short respite of a fortnight, we were now back in the position of having to play six games (commencing with the match against Newcastle) in three weeks, so after the game against Bury we travelled to Charlton for the fixture the following Saturday.

Charlton occupied a lowly position in the league and were really struggling, but whatever they lacked on the field, they were not without optimism off it because I was greeted by one of their players, Sammy Lawrie, with the news that the second half of the game was to be broadcast.

They always won, Sammy said, when under the ear of the nation.

I told Sammy jokingly that under the circumstances we would keep our scoring to a single goal in the first half, reserving our real efforts for the second period so that our own fans could have the opportunity of hearing us win handsomely.

Strangely enough, this is exactly the way the scoring went. The first half was a hard one, with very little between the sides as far as play went and it was obvious to me that Charlton had talent in their side, but the ball was running against them.

Halfway through the second half, which had been even to this point, we scored again. This seemed to increase the team's confidence, so much so that they began to slow down the pace of the game, much to the annoyance of the Charlton supporters, who immediately assumed we were trying to 'take the mickey' out of the Charlton boys.

I can assure them that this was not the case and if they want proof then I would point out to them that following two of these three slowed down movements, we scored goals.

Although we won by a handsome margin, I can say with all honesty that Charlton were decidedly unlucky to be beaten by such a score, but at the same time I must give credit to our boys for the

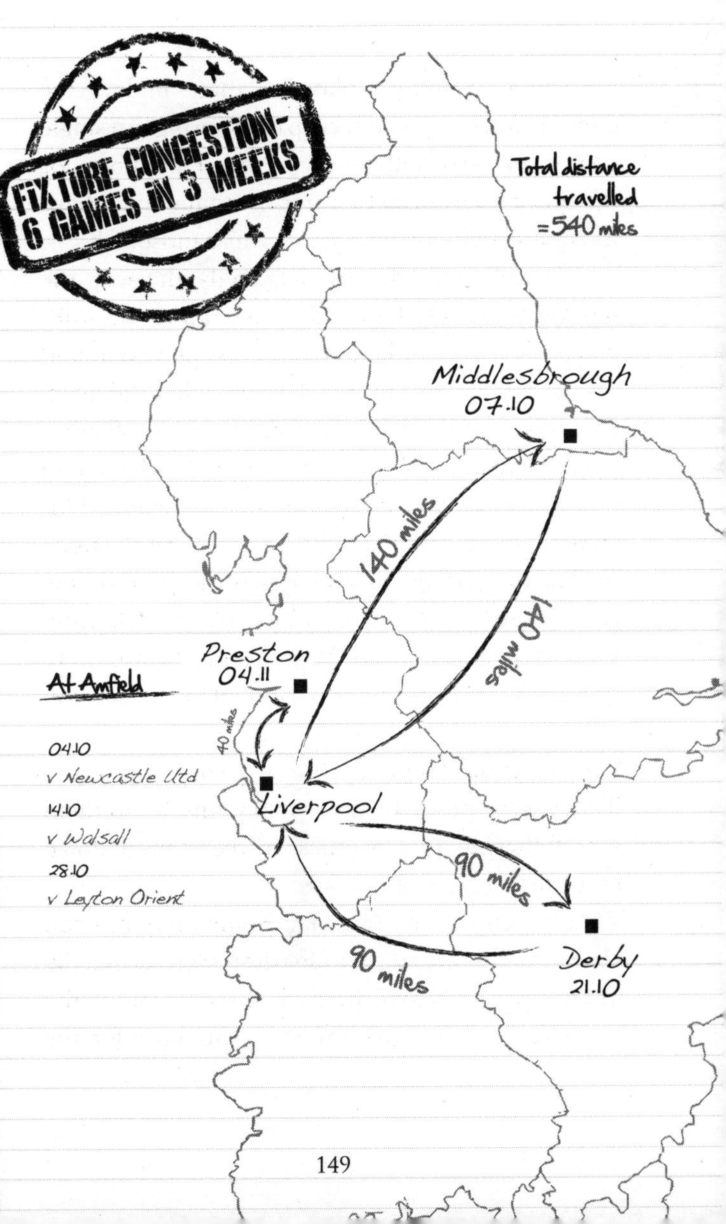
FIXTURE CONGESTION-
6 GAMES IN 3 WEEKS
Total distance
travelled
=540 miles
Middlesbrough
07.10
140 miles
140 miles
Preston
04.11
40 miles
At Anfield
04.10
v Newcastle Utd
14.10
v Walsall
28.10
v Leyton Orient
Liverpool
90 miles
90 miles
Derby
21.10

SECOND DIVISION
30.09.1961
THE VALLEY

Manager		Manager	
James Trotter		Bill Shankly	
CHARLTON ATH	 0	LIVERPOOL	 4

1	William Duff	1	Bert Slater
2	John Dav Sewell	2	Dick White
3	Don Townsend	3	Gerry Byrne
4	John D Hewie	4	Gordon Milne
5	Marvin Hinton	5	Ron Yeats
6	Michael Bailey	6	Tommy Leishman
7	Sam Lawrie	7	Kevin Lewis
8	Ron White	8	Roger Hunt
9	Dennis Edwards	9	Ian St John
10	Fred Lucas	10	Jimmy Melia
11	Brian Kinsey	11	Alan A'Court

Attendance:- 14,236

Goals:- Hunt 44, 78
Lewis 82
St John 84

brand of football which they played, which continued our successful run.

This had brought our total to ten games without loss and we had begun to realise that there was a lot of truth in what the Scunthorpe official said about being beaten sometime.

Still, it had not happened to date and everybody was determined that the day on which it did should be postponed for as long as possible.

Anxiety And Relief

We gathered at Melwood on the Monday for routine training for our second clash with Newcastle, a game which, with our unbeaten record plus the added attraction of Ivor Allchurch in the Newcastle forwards, was going to bring a huge crowd through the turnstiles. I was right in my judgement because the crowd of 52,419 witnessed a great game.

Our assessment of Newcastle was that they were a far better team than their position in the league table indicated and everybody who saw this particular match will, I am sure, agree with this opinion.

It was an extremely hard game with no quarter

SECOND DIVISION
04.10.1961
ANFIELD

Manager		Manager	
Bill Shankly		Norman Smith	
LIVERPOOL	2 	NEWCASTLE	0 
1	Bert Slater	1	Dave Hollins
2	Dick White	2	Bill McKinney
3	Gerry Byrne	3	Alf McMichael
4	Gordon Milne	4	Duncan Neale
5	Ron Yeats	5	George Heslop
6	Tommy Leishman	6	George Dalton
7	Kevin Lewis	7	Gordon Hughes
8	Roger Hunt	8	Ivor Allchurch
9	Ian St John	9	Len White
10	Jimmy Melia	10	Johnny McGuigan
11	Alan A'Court	11	Liam Tuohy

Goals:- Lewis 38
Hunt 75

Attendance:- 52,419

asked or given. In Allchurch, Newcastle have a wonderful inside-forward and ball player. As far as our boys were concerned, it would be invidious to pick out any for special mention.

Although the game, result and spectacle was a great success, there was one aspect of it which gave me a lot of anxiety. This was an injury to Ronnie Yeats.

Early in the game he had gone up for a high ball and had fallen awkwardly on his right shoulder. He was in a lot of pain for the rest of the match, although spectators cannot have known this because he still managed to play well.

The shoulder was so intensely sensitive to the touch that it crossed my mind that he had sustained a fracture and if this turned out to be the case, it could have the most serious repercussions on our future programme.

Even if the injury turned out to be less serious than at first seemed likely, it did not seem possible for him to be fit in time for our game against Middlesbrough on the following Saturday.

This in itself would be relatively serious because Dick White was suffering from an aggravating knee injury and Ian St John had been given leave to play for his country against Ireland.

	Team	P	W	D	L	F	A	Pts	GA
1	Liverpool	11	10	1	0	31	4	21	7.75
2	Southampton	11	6	2	3	21	10	14	2.10
3	Rotherham United	10	7	0	3	23	18	14	1.28
4	Derby County	11	6	1	4	24	23	13	1.04
5	Leyton Orient	11	5	2	4	20	13	12	1.54
6	Huddersfield Town	11	5	2	4	20	18	12	1.11
7	Luton Town	11	6	0	5	26	24	12	1.08
8	Plymouth Argyle	11	5	2	4	16	18	12	0.89
9	Bury	11	6	0	5	16	19	12	0.84
10	Walsall	11	5	2	4	16	19	112	0.84
11	Scunthorpe United	11	4	3	4	25	23	11	1.09
12	Sunderland	11	5	1	5	22	22	11	1.00
13	Norwich City	11	4	3	4	18	18	11	1.00
14	Brighton & H A	11	3	5	3	15	17	11	0.88
15	Swansea Town	11	2	6	3	20	25	10	0.80
16	Stocke City	11	3	3	5	18	17	9	1.06
17	Middlesbrough	10	3	3	4	19	19	9	1.00
18	Newcastle United	11	3	2	6	10	13	8	0.77
19	Preston North End	11	3	2	6	14	19	8	0.74
20	Bristol Rovers	11	3	1	7	14	20	7	0.70
21	Leeds United	11	3	1	7	11	22	7	0.50
22	Charlton Athletic	11	1	2	8	11	29	4	0.38

Thus, after playing the same team for eleven consecutive games, it seemed possible that we might have to make three changes.

Yeats reported early at the ground the following morning and for all the sleep he had been able to get, he could just as easily have reported in the middle of the night.

However, Bob Paisley and I took him to see a specialist and never were fingers crossed more securely than Bob's and mine whilst the examination was in progress and the x-rays taken and scrutinised.

This took a couple of hours and then, to our great relief, the diagnosis was given as very severe bruising with no signs of fracture.

The fact that he would be a very doubtful starter for this Middlesbrough game seemed almost good news in comparison with what we feared would be the verdict.

* * * * *

"My feeling was that if ever a team deserved success, then that team was Liverpool. This was the text of my sermons to the boys during the start of the next week and by the time Saturday arrived, one had the feeling that the loss of two points had been forgotten."

A First Defeat

I finished my last article at a point where, after the sun had shone brightly on the Liverpool club for 11 matches, quite suddenly black clouds loomed on the horizon and it looked as though a storm might burst upon us.

Ronnie Yeats had sustained a shoulder injury which seemed certain to keep him out of the team for our next match against Middlesbrough, Dick White had a damaged knee, which while not sufficiently bad to stop him training, was causing increasing anxiety because of the possibility of it 'blowing up' suddenly, and Ian St John had been released for international duty on the day the Middlesbrough fixture was to be played.

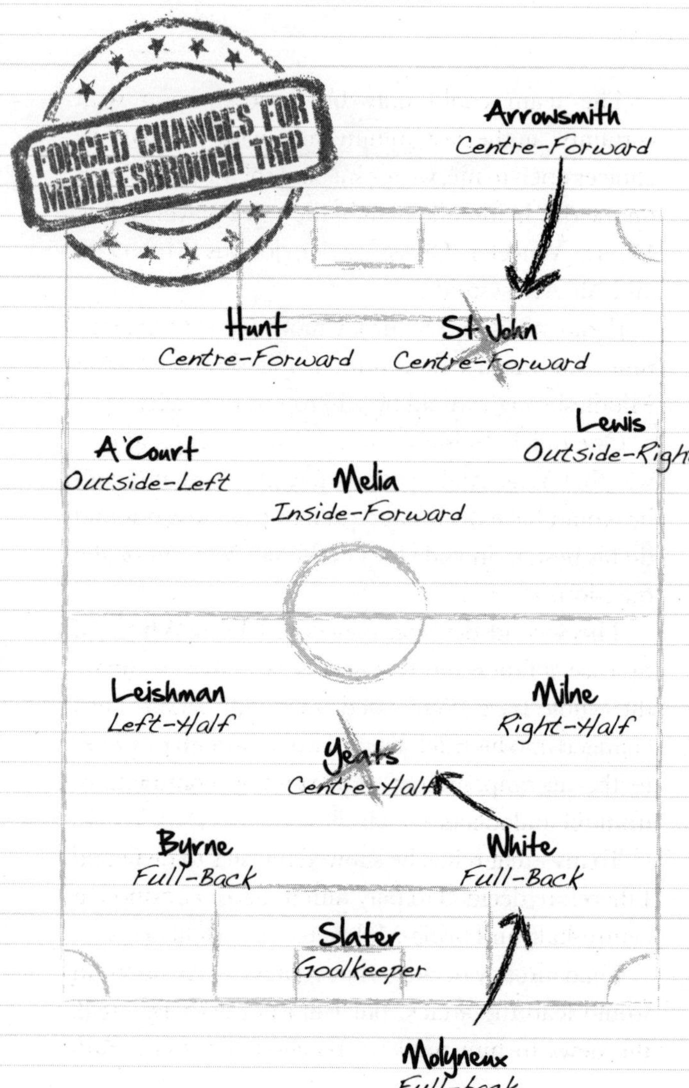
FORCED CHANGES FOR MIDDLESBROUGH TRIP
Arrowsmith
Centre-Forward
Hunt
Centre-Forward
St John
Centre-Forward
Lewis
Outside-Right
A'Court
Outside-Left
Melia
Inside-Forward
Leishman
Left-Half
Milne
Right-Half
Yeats
Centre-Half
Byrne
Full-Back
White
Full-Back
Slater
Goalkeeper
Molyneux
Full-back

The team could only be decided upon with certainty at the last minute and with the various choices open to me, we took a party of 14 to Saltburn on the day before the match, the extra players being Johnny Wheeler, Chris Lawler, Johnny Molyneux and Alf Arrowsmith.

Friday night and Saturday morning were anxious times for me, as even with a full side I felt that Middlesbrough would be a hard nut to crack.

One quick decision was made first thing and that was that Yeats could not possibly play and although he would have been quite prepared to turn out and do his best, to include him in the side was out of the question.

The second decision concerned Dick White. In his case, a fitness test was necessary and accordingly the whole party descended upon the bench, Dick changed into his tracksuit and went through his paces to the accompaniment of a running commentary from the onlookers.

To my great relief, he showed himself to be fit and I therefore decided to play him in his old position at centre-half and bring Molyneux in at right-back.

I had already decided that young Alf Arrowsmith would lead the attack, but I did not actually break the news to him until we reached Ayresome Park as I did not want him to feel worried about his responsibilities. Worry can only drain more from a player than actually playing a hard game.

Of the 14 players who travelled in the party, those not in the side were Yeats, Wheeler and Lawler. The latter is a very promising centre-half of whom I have the highest hopes in the future and if White had proved to be unfit, I would have played Chris at centre-half with the sure knowledge that he would not let us down.

However, under the particular set of circumstances prevailing, I felt that Dick's great experience made him an automatic choice. Lawler's chance was only deferred.

The result of the match is now in the history books. In a game which never reached any great heights, we lost 2-0, the only scorer being the unfortunate White with two own goals, although in fairness to young Arrowsmith (who gave everything he had for all of the game), it must be recorded that in this, his first senior match, he scored twice. One of these was clearly offside, but for some mysterious reason the referee declined to allow the other.

Well there it was; we had lost our first match, which at first seemed to everybody like an acute blow. However, once we had left the ground, we

SECOND DIVISION
07.10.1961
AYRESOME PARK

Manager	Manager
Robert Dennison	Bill Shankly

MIDDLESBROUGH  LIVERPOOL 

	Middlesbrough		Liverpool
1	Bob Appleby	1	Bert Slater
2	Derek Stonehouse	2	John Molyneux
3	Mick McNeil	3	Gerry Byrne
4	Ray Yeoman	4	Gordon Milne
5	Bill Gates	5	Dick White
6	Dick Neal	6	Tommy Leishman
7	Bill Harris	7	Kevin Lewis
8	Arthur Kaye	8	Roger Hunt
9	Alan Peacock	9	Alf Arrowsmith
10	Billy Horner	10	Jimmy Melia
11	Edwin Holliday	11	Alan A'Court

Goals:- White o/g 49
White o/g 64

Attendance:- 23,780

had the matter in its true perspective, which was that we had a wonderful start to the season and lost only when fielding a much weakened side. Nobody could grumble and I am sure nobody did.

Middlesbrough had the privilege of being our first conquerors. At the same time, the win had relieved the tension under which the team had been labouring, a tension which had built up progressively as the season advanced.

Now this was gone and our task was to get back into our normal stride and not allow this minor setback to affect our confidence.

Back At Full Strength

My feeling was that if ever a team deserved success, then that team was Liverpool. This was the text of my sermons to the boys during the start of the next week and by the time Saturday arrived, one had the feeling that the loss of two points had been forgotten.

With the return of St John after his international duty and Yeats once more fit again, we were at full strength for the visit of Walsall to Anfield.

Walsall was one of the newly promoted sides from the Third Division. They appeared to be a team with fluctuating form, but on the whole, I did not think we should have much difficulty winning on our own ground.

The first half was a hard-fought affair and I was astonished when we suddenly found ourselves one down, Yeats having deflected a ball out of Slater's reach.

However, Lewis quickly equalised and this concluded the scoring in what had been an excellent first period in which Walsall had given a really good account of themselves.

The second half was too much for the visitors. When the boys really turned on the heat, the pace proved too much for them.

The team played straight-forward, aggressive football with no frills, which would have beaten teams with a far greater reputation than that possessed by the visitors, and scored another five goals.

I heard after the game that both the Walsall team and their officials were completely nonplussed by our exhibition in the second half.

It is interesting to note that, at this time, we had scored 37 goals and conceded only seven. Of this seven, no less than four had been given away by our own centre-halves, two being credited to White and two to Yeats.

SECOND DIVISION
14.10.1961
ANFIELD

Manager		Manager	
Bill Shankly		William Moore	
LIVERPOOL	6	WALSALL	1

	Liverpool		Walsall
1	Bert Slater	1	Keith Ball
2	Dick White	2	Grenville Palin
3	Gerry Byrne	3	John Sharples
4	Gordon Milne	4	Ken Hill
5	Ron Yeats	5	Albert McPherson
6	Tommy Leishman	6	Jimmy Dudley
7	Kevin Lewis	7	George Meek
8	Roger Hunt	8	Ken Hodgkinson
9	Ian St John	9	Tommy Wilson
10	Jimmy Melia	10	Tony Richards
11	Alan A'Court	11	Colin Taylor

Goals:- Lewis 41
Melia 47
Hunt 50, 57, 80
St John 61

Goal:- Yeats o/g 23

Attendance:- 42,229

Thus, we had quickly put behind us the memory of our only defeat and were back on the winning trail again.

The Derby, Derby And The Orient

This brought us to the friendly match against our old friends and foes from across the park. Did I say 'friendly?' Is it possible to have such a match between these two sides?

Anyway, for want of a better phrase, it passed as a friendly and was played before a crowd of 60,000 at Goodison under lights. Where else in Britain could there be such an atmosphere, Celtic and Rangers apart, and where else would a crowd turn out for a friendly?

It is not necessary for me to go into detail of what was a great game, but for the record, Roger Hunt scored twice and for Everton Bobby Collins and Roy Vernon (penalty) replied.

Everyone who witnessed this game must have been satisfied with the fare served and the result was a good one with honour satisfied for both sides.

On the Saturday following this midweek 'derby',

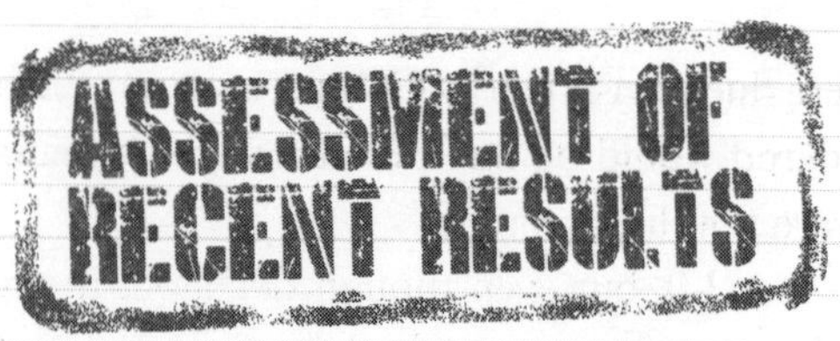

Match summary

Opposition	Comments
18.10.1961 **v Everton** Floodlit Challenge Cup – 2nd Leg Goodison Park	Impressive crowd of 60,000 for return 'friendly' at Goodison Park. Two goals from Hunt cancelled out by replies from Everton's Collins and a penalty from Vernon. Good standard of football to please spectators. Result: Drew 2–2
21.10.1961 **v Derby County** Second Division Baseball Ground	As expected, a tough game but exertions against Everton in midweek may account for the defeat suffered here, but generally no complaints. Team still performed well. Result: Lost 2–0
28.10.1961 **v Leyton Orient** Second Division Anfield	Johnny Carey's side pose greatest threat in promotion race as confirmed by this 3–3 result. Indeed, we were fortunate to share the points. Two goals from Hunt and one from Leishman matched by two-goal salvo from the impressive Dunmore, Foster finding the other. Result: Drew 3–3

we were due to visit Derby County, a game which we considered would be one of our toughest matches. We were not disappointed.

We lost 2-0, but even though defeated, the team played well, although one had the feeling that their efforts against Everton had taken a bit of the edge off them. However, there were no complaints.

We trained all week in preparation for the visit to Anfield of Johnny Carey's new team, Leyton Orient. In the past few seasons Liverpool and the Orient had some wonderful games, of which the one that comes most readily to mind is the cup tie in which Roger Hunt won the game for Liverpool in the dying seconds of what had been a first-class match.

If the previous games against Leyton set a high standard, this one undoubtedly maintained it. For a long time our record of having not lost a match at Anfield was in jeopardy against a side which has one of the best defensive records in England, and in addition a forward line which is led by the clever Dave Dunmore.

My assessment of the Leyton club was that, under the guidance of the very shrewd Johnny Carey, they were going to be Liverpool's greatest rival in the promotion race.

The game ended in a 3-3 draw and, to be perfectly honest, I thought we were lucky to share the points.

Going 'Home' For Cally's Debut

Our next match was against Preston North End and to go there was, for me, like returning home after a long visit away because it was here that I spent 16 years as a player.

A match against any Lancashire club is almost a local derby and naturally there was this added incentive to win – apart form my personal anxiety to do well against my old club at Deepdale.

This game saw the first change in our line-up (apart from those brought about by injury or international calls) since the opening day of the season.

Young Ian Callaghan had, from the start of the season, been putting up consistently sterling performances in the Central League side, so much so that he forced his way into the first team on the right wing instead of Kevin Lewis.

We travelled to Preston with the biggest crowd of supporters that had attended any away game

SECOND DIVISION
04.11.1961
DEEPDALE

Manager James Milne		Manager Bill Shankly	
PRESTON N.E	 1	LIVERPOOL	 3
1	Alan Kelly	1	Bert Slater
2	Willie Cunningham	2	Dick White
3	George Ross	3	Gerry Byrne
4	John Wylie	4	Gordon Milne
5	Tony Singleton	5	Ron Yeats
6	Dave Barber	6	Tommy Leishman
7	Alec Alston	7	Ian Callaghan
8	Alfie Biggs	8	Roger Hunt
9	Alex Dawson	9	Ian St John
10	David Sneddon	10	Jimmy Melia
11	Peter Thompson	11	Alan A'Court

Goal:- Sneddon

Goals:- Milne 29
Callaghan 56
St John 63

Attendance:- 29,243

up to that point and when we eventually arrived at Deepdale, I felt certain that there were more Liverpool than Preston supporters.

This kind of following is of the greatest value to the team and we must have pleased those who made the journey by our form. We won 3-1.

Ironically enough, our scoring was opened by Gordon Milne, whose father manages the Preston club.

I felt that 19-year-old Callaghan fully justified his place, as apart from marking his debut with a goal, his play throughout was of a high order.

I had considered that Preston, a team just relegated from the First Division, would be a stiff hurdle to negotiate and we were therefore extremely pleased to leave with both points in the bag.

Leaving Preston was not an easy task because it seemed that every Liverpool supporter had travelled to Preston in his own car and the number of vehicles created a traffic jam worse than the one which was to occur later in the season when we were travelling to Preston to play them in the cup.

I mention this incident because it crossed my mind at the time that if we succeed in our efforts to get back into the First Division, then we could expect to spend a large amount of our travelling time next season in traffic jams because of the number of Lancashire teams in the First Division.

This, however, was something which we were prepared to accept; indeed, the thought of all these added supporters was an inspiration to us.

*****

"Our goal tally for 19 matches was over the 50 mark with only 15 against us and as we were approaching the halfway stage, the outlook was really beginning to look bright and we were being talked about as a racing certainty for promotion."

Vultures Seeking Their Prey

Following our away fixture against Preston came a home game against Luton, a rather undistinguished side whom we should not have had much difficulty in beating.

Roger Hunt was unfit and I had brought in Kevin Lewis to partner Ian Callaghan on the right wing. However, the best we could manage was a draw and this result left me really angry.

It was not so much dropping a point to a mediocre side and their scrambling a doubtful goal in the dying minutes of the game and then our having a bed-rock claim for a penalty disallowed in the last few seconds.

For the first time during the season, I really boiled

over at a result, not at the team, but at the thought of losing a valuable point in a game which we should have won by three or four clear goals.

It took a few days for me to even think about this match without getting angry, but eventually I consoled myself with the thought that this was football and the good would eventually balance out the bad.

Following this game, a number of players were taken to Blackpool for a few days special training, a procedure which I considered would be beneficial at this stage of the season.

Our next game was against Huddersfield and it, therefore, had a double interest for me; we wanted the points and I wanted to do well against the club which I had managed immediately prior to my coming at Anfield.

A visit to this Yorkshire club is never an easy one and this game proved to be no exception. We won 2-1 and our forward display in the first half which pierced the Huddersfield defence repeatedly was of the highest order. Possibly the spacious ground suited our style of play.

This brought our total number of wins for away matches up to seven and in considering our overall position, I found this a comfortable thought because

OUR CURRENT AWAY RECORD COMPARED TO TEAMS WHO RECENTLY WON PROMOTION

		P	W	D	L	F	A	GA	Pts
1961–62	Liverpool	10	7	1	2	19	9	2.11	15

Teams promoted to First Division – Away record only

	Team	P	W	D	L	F	A	GA	Pts
1960–61	Ipswich Town	21	11	4	6	45	31	1.45	26
	Sheffield United	21	10	4	7	32	29	1.10	24
1959–60	Aston Villa	21	8	6	7	27	24	1.12	22
	Cardiff City	21	8	10	3	35	26	1.35	26
1958–59	Sheffield Weds	21	10	4	7	38	35	1.09	24
	Fulham	21	9	5	7	31	35	0.89	23
1957–58	West Ham Utd	21	11	3	7	45	29	1.55	25
	Blackburn Rovers	21	9	5	7	43	39	1.10	23
1956–57	Leicester City	21	11	6	4	41	31	1.32	28
	Nottingham Forest	21	9	6	6	44	26	1.69	24
1955–56	Sheffield Weds	21	8	8	5	41	34	1.21	24
	Leeds United	21	6	3	12	29	42	0.69	15
1954–55	Birmingham City	21	8	6	7	36	25	1.44	22
	Luton Town	21	5	6	10	33	35	0.94	16

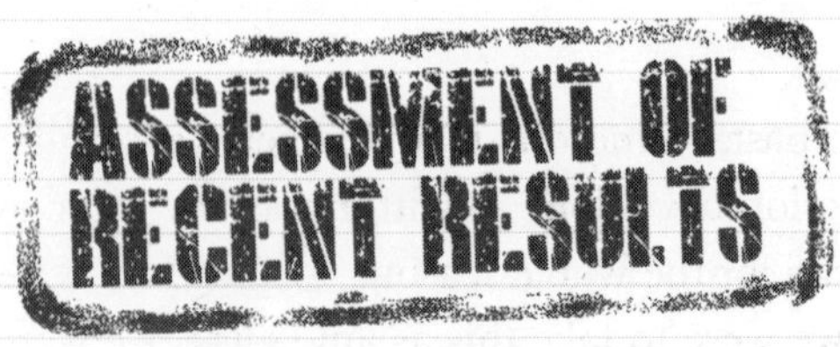

Match summary

Opposition	Comments
11.11.1961 **v Luton Town** Second Division Anfield	Disappointing result!! Valuable point conceded to a mediocre team. Should have won by three or four goals. Not helped by conceding a dubious late goal and having a concrete claim for a penalty waved away. Very angry! Result: Drew 1-1!
18.11.1961 **v Huddersfield Tn** Second Division Leeds Road	Happy return to former club. Not an easy place to visit but our forwards dismantled the Huddersfield defence in a first half which brought a goal apiece for Melia and Hunt. Result: Won 2-1
25.11.1961 **v Swansea Town** Second Division Anfield	Both sides at a stalemate in tough and even first half. Different story after the break as we hammered home five goals much to the amazement of the Swansea officials. Melia got us off the mark with first two followed by a hat-trick from Hunt. Pair of vultures! Result: Won 5-0

in the past, numerous teams which have achieved promotion have done so with not many more away victories for the whole season.

If we were to take this as any guide, we were on our way to Division One. Wins against such teams as we had already beaten had charged the team with confidence and the freedom from injury which we had so far experienced was a real god-send.

Following the win against Huddersfield, we prepared for the visit of Anfield of Swansea Town, a club which has, in the past, provided many Welsh internationals and was quite capable of putting up a good show against the best.

The first half was hard and as even as the nil-nil score suggests. The second half gave the impression that the boys had used the first period merely to tire the opposition for they turned on a show similar to that in the second half against Walsall, and again scored five goals.

I well remember a Swansea official's words to me after the game: "I was really glad when the game was over; even in the closing stages your players were like vultures seeking their prey."

The director in question meant goals when he talked about 'prey' and he added that he found the second half quite shattering.

Sick At Southampton

Our goal tally for 19 matches was over the 50 mark with only 15 against us and as we were approaching the halfway stage, the outlook was really beginning to look bright and we were being talked about as a racing certainty for promotion.

However, we were not to be misled by idle talk and did not look too far into the future, our policy being to treat each game as it came along as the most important match of the season – as indeed it was.

We met Southampton the following week and for this fixture we flew into Southampton on a murky December day, on which the pilot had the greatest difficulty finding the airfield which was without laid runways.

Ronnie Yeats' weakness again caught up with him. This is air-sickness, particularly during the period of descent.

The second half of this match was broadcast and, as it turned out, would have been impossible to have picked a better game for this purpose, the standard of football being easily worthy of Division One.

Both points went to the opposition, the score being two-nil, but this could so easily have been the other way about. At that time, Southampton were being looked upon as Liverpool's bogey team – and so they were.

However, we were not to know that their return fixture against us would prove to be such an historic occasion in the club's history and the bogey would be well and truly laid.

We flew back to Liverpool and landed at about 8pm. Whether one likes flying or not, the fact that one can be home from a game played over 200 miles away in three hours after the final whistle provides a fact against which it is difficult to find any suitable argument.

Following the setback at Southampton, we entertained Plymouth Argyle in a match which once again proved to be above the normal standard and I thought we were rather fortunate to take both points.

The Plymouth right-half Johnny Williams dominated the game, constantly prompting attacks and the whole side played top-class football.

The next game was against the lowly-placed Bristol Rovers, against whom we had opened the season, and the result of a game which I recollect as noteworthy more for its ruggedness than for its brilliance, and we collected another couple of points.

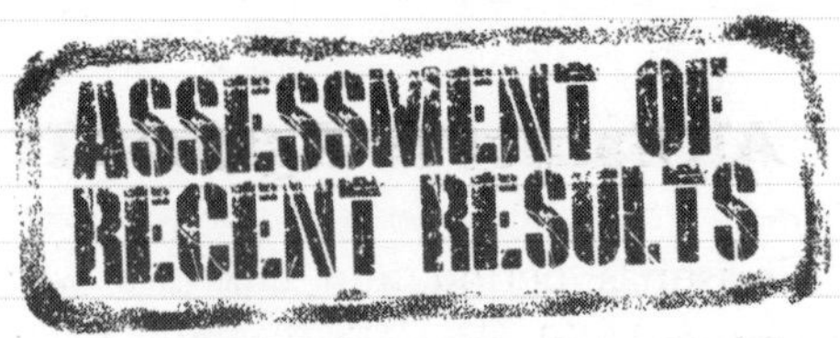

Match summary

Opposition	Comments
02.12.1961 **v Southampton** Second Division The Dell	Hugely entertaining; easily up to the standard of Division One football. But our bogey team strike again with a goal in either half Result: Lost 2-0
09.12.1961 **v Plymouth Argyle** Second Division Anfield	Well contested and played to a high standard. Visitors difficult to control, their right-half especially problematic. Lucky to win through goals from A'Court and St John. Result: Won 2-1
16.12.1961 **v Bristol Rovers** Second Division Anfield	A rugged contest against Bert Tann's team called for more substance than style. St John and Hunt the goalscorers. Result: Won 2-0
23.12.1961 **v Leeds United** Elland Road	Frozen and dangerous pitches, like playing on an ice rink! Neither game should have gone ahead. Results: Lost both games 1-0!
26.12.1961 **v Rotherham Utd** Millmoor	

All Sanity Is Against It

The Christmas period and cup ties were now imminent and with the arrival of this time, about halfway through the season, our main concern was to prevent staleness and complacency creeping in.

This period is always a trying time for managers of football clubs. Parties are held to which players are invited and it does not take a lot of Christmas fare to upset the fitness of an athlete, which I am sure accounts for the odd results which, for time immemorial, have occurred about this time of year.

From these remarks I would not like it to be implied that we lost our games at Leeds and Rotherham because members of the team had too many parties, because nothing could be further from the truth.

Both these games were played on grounds which resembled skating rinks and training on skates was possibly the only item of preparation for the season which we had not undertaken.

As I am sure the opposition in both cases had not undertaken it either, there was a great element of luck about these games under the conditions in which they were played, and the luck was not in our favour.

I have long held the opinion that no game of any importance should be played on grounds in such a state. All sanity is against it.

Spectators pay to see good play which is out of the question under these conditions, and from the players' point of view, the risk of injury is out of all magnitude by comparison with the ordinary game.

At Rotherham, Ronnie Yeats took a toss which, on a normal pitch, would have had no ill-effects whatsoever, but on the ice-bound ground on which we were playing he sprained a wrist severely and broke a bone in his hand.

When I saw him fall I thought he must have broke his neck and I was more than relieved to see him get to his feet again.

This problem of frozen pitches is something which has yet to be solved. Everton made a brave and expensive attempt to do it but the effect on the pitch in conditions other than frost gave them no option but to abandon the scheme.

Murrayfield, the headquarters of rugby union in Scotland, have a system of underground electrical wiring which, I understand, has proved a great success, but the amount of play this ground receives is nothing like as great as that on a league soccer ground, so that help is received from the grass covered turf.

In this day and age it seems fantastic that the best method which can be devised is the oldest, that of straw covered pitches; there is certainly room for science to move in this matter and money for the man who can produce a workable scheme.

Bonetti Wondered What Had Happened To Him

Following the reverses against Leeds and Rotherham, we were due to commence 1962 with a cup tie at home to Chelsea, a club fighting to keep off the bottom of the First Division.

If one were to consider the two divisions as one, they were very close to us by virtue of our own position at the top of Division Two and it appeared to everybody a most attractive fixture with the result that 48,000 spectators saw the game, and what an amazing game it turned out to be.

From the start of the match, the noise was deafening, but as we knew that most of it was from our own supporters, it was of the greatest encouragement to the team.

FA CUP 3RD RND
06.01.1962
ANFIELD

Manager		Manager	
Bill Shankly		Tommy Docherty	
LIVERPOOL	4 	CHELSEA	3 
1	Bert Slater	1	Peter Bonetti
2	John Molyneux	2	Ken Shellito
3	Gerry Byrne	3	Allan Harris
4	Gordon Milne	4	Andy Malcolm
5	Ron Yeats	5	Allan Young
6	Tommy Leishman	6	Mel Scott
7	Ian Callaghan	7	Peter Brabrook
8	Roger Hunt	8	Bobby Tambling
9	Ian St John	9	Barry Bridges
10	Jimmy Melia	10	Bert Murray
11	Alan A'Court	11	Frank Blunstone

Goals:- St John 16, 41
Hunt 28
A'Court 44

Goals:- Tambling 18, 67
Bridges 76

Attendance:- 48,455

In heavy going, we had a wonderful first half and were leading 4-1 at the interval, but when I say that the score could have easily been double this figure, you can imagine the fireworks which had taken place in the Chelsea goal area.

Young Bonetti must have wondered what happened to him with our forwards peppering from the front and the Kop keeping up an incessant roar at his back; if any man was glad to hear the whistle at half-time, surely it was the Chelsea keeper.

The second half was a different story. We relaxed just a little and in doing so allowed Chelsea to get away with two silly goals and they were suddenly back in the game. However, this completed the scoring, so their fight-back was insufficient for them to earn a replay and we were through to round four.

After this match, a number of players were again taken to Blackpool for special training and a general tonic for the strenuous months ahead.

A week later, our supporters were again treated to a feast of goals when we beat Norwich 5-4. From first to last, this was an interesting game and in the closing stages, having scored five goals, we very nearly dropped a point.

The next side against which we were attempting

a double was Scunthorpe; we had beaten them at Anfield in September by the odd goal in three.

We had to be content with a draw, a result which left us with a good deal of dissatisfaction because it seemed to everybody but the referee that Roger Hunt had scored a brilliant goal which was disallowed.

We have to accept these things and as I have said before, over a season I suppose that they even themselves, but at a time when every point is a vital one, they are keenly felt when the decision is against you.

*****

LEAGUE STANDINGS JAN 20TH 1962...

	Team	P	W	D	L	F	A	Pts	GA
1	Liverpool	26	17	4	5	61	25	38	2.44
2	Leyton Orient	26	16	5	5	52	25	37	2.08
3	Southampton	27	13	6	8	51	38	32	1.34
4	Rotherham United	25	12	6	7	52	48	30	1.08
5	Derby County	27	12	6	9	53	49	30	1.08
6	Plymouth Argyle	27	12	6	9	48	46	30	1.04
7	Sunderland	26	12	5	9	53	38	29	1.39
8	Scunthorpe United	25	11	6	8	55	46	28	1.26
9	Stoke City	26	11	6	9	40	34	28	1.18
10	Luton Town	26	12	3	11	53	45	27	1.18
11	Walsall	25	10	5	10	40	44	25	0.91
12	Norwich City	27	9	7	11	43	54	25	0.80
13	Preston North End	27	9	6	12	34	40	24	0.85
14	Huddersfield Town	25	8	7	10	38	38	23	1.00
15	Swansea Town	26	7	8	11	38	58	22	0.66
16	Bury	25	10	2	13	34	53	22	0.64
17	Brighton & H A	26	7	8	11	29	52	22	0.56
18	Newcastle United	25	7	7	11	41	36	21	1.14
19	Leeds United	25	8	5	12	32	43	21	0.74
20	Middlesbrough	25	7	5	13	46	51	19	0.90
21	Bristol Rovers	27	8	2	17	34	54	18	0.63
22	Charlton Athletic	24	6	5	13	35	48	17	0.73

"The possibility of us having a reasonable run in the cup had fired the imagination of our supporters, and this brought home to me the responsibility which we were carrying to justify the good-will of these fans."

Anfield Cup Fever

After the away match against Scunthorpe, we reached Anfield about 9.30pm. Instead of the place being deserted, we discovered the start of a queue for tickets for the cup tie against Oldham Athletic.

This brought to mind memories of the queues which used to wait all night to secure tickets for Preston's pre-War cup games and of the scenes in Glasgow for matches which involved Scotland or Celtic and Rangers, when Sauchiehall Street would be packed all night.

Watching these enthusiasts settle down for their long wait emphasised the way which our success in the league and the possibility of us having a reasonable run in the cup had fired the imagination of our supporters, and this brought home to me the responsibility which we were carrying to justify the good-will of these fans.

I know that everybody connected with the club had the same feeling and it made the team more determined to be worthy of this great enthusiasm.

In spite of the fact that Oldham are in Division Four, we treated them with the same respect which we gave all opponents. Having played in many FA Cup games against similar opposition, I knew that we were in for a battle...and a battle it turned out to be. In the end we won 2-1, but knew that we had been in a match!

All thoughts were now concentrated upon the draw for the 5th round, and we found ourselves again paired with Lancashire neighbours, this time Preston.

For me, this was a strange draw indeed, as in my playing days, I appeared in no less than 35 consecutive cup ties for North End. For a club with headquarters in a comparatively small place, they had proved themselves to be one of the leading cup fighters in the country and I knew that we had something really hot on our plate.

From the cup back to the league and we had Brighton as our next visitors to Anfield. This match

Fifth Round

Aston Villa (div 1) v Charlton Athletic (div 2)

Blackburn Rovers (div 1) v Middlesbrough (div 2)

Burnley (div 1) v Everton (div 1)

Fulham (div 1) v Port Vale (div 3)

Liverpool (div 2) v Preston North End (div 2)

Manchester United (div 1) v Sheffield Wednesday (div 1)

Sheffield United (div 1) v Norwich City (div)

West Bromwich Albion (div 1) v Tottenham Hotspur (div 1)

SECOND DIVISION
03.02.1962
ANFIELD

Manager		Manager	
Bill Shankly		George Curtis	
LIVERPOOL	3	BRIGHTON	1

	Liverpool		Brighton
1	Bert Slater	1	Charlie Baker
2	Gerry Byrne	2	Bob McNichol
3	Ronnie Moran	3	Bobby Baxter
4	Gordon Milne	4	Jack Bertolini
5	Ron Yeats	5	Roy Jennings
6	Tommy Leishman	6	Steve Burtenshaw
7	Ian Callaghan	7	Mike Tiddy
8	Roger Hunt	8	Ian McNeill
9	Ian St John	9	Tony Sitford
10	Jimmy Melia	10	Tony Nicholas
11	Alan A'Court	11	Johnny Goodchild

Goals:- Byrne 52
Hunt 81
St John 87

Goal:- Sitford

Attendance:- 36,414

saw the reintroduction of Ronnie Moran as left-back with Gerry Byrne moving to the right. This change was made necessary by an injury to Dick White in the Oldham game.

As events transpired, Dick had played in his last game for the club, but the many fine exhibitions and good sportsmanship of this great-hearted player have earned the thanks of all our supporters.

We got an awful shock in the opening seconds of this game when Stitford, the Brighton centre-forward, scrambled a goal. This was the sign for the whole of the Brighton side to drop back in defence and we had the greatest difficulty in beating this lowly-placed team.

Tactics such as these, although no doubt employed in light of their desperate position in the table, do nothing to attract the crowds to football grounds.

The other point of interest which emphasises the way in which Brighton packed their goal area, was that our scoring was opened by Gerry Byrne with a long lob that deceived the Brighton keeper.

The following week we visited Bury and leading their attack was Dave Hickson who had left Anfield to go to Bury via Cambridge.

The team were able to saunter through this in a way which made football look easy and we won by three clear goals, all scored by Roger Hunt, who thus brought his tally of goals to 28.

Our preparation for the cup tie against Preston was undertaken at home. Perhaps the fact that we had already beaten them this term made us a bit too sure of ourselves, but if this is so, then we got a severe shock because in front of 55,000 spectators, we were held to a goalless draw. We were, in fact, nearly beaten.

In spite of the fact that all at Anfield were far more interested in the league than the cup, we were disappointed in this result but knew that we had a stiff game facing us in the replay.

Never Has There Been Such An Exodus To See An Away Game

I will never forget the crowds which queued round the ground on the Sunday morning to get their tickets for this game at Deepdale. The scenes were truly amazing and once again I was reminded of the tremendous importance of Liverpool FC to our supporters and of our responsibility to them.

If the scenes on Sunday were impressive, they were nothing in comparison with those which took place on the day of the match.

Having been assured by the police of an escort from Aintree to Deepdale, we took it for granted that we should have ample time if we left Anfield at 5.45pm, and so we should had it not been for our faithful supporters.

In the history of the club, never has there been such an exodus from the city to see an away game. It would be interesting to know how many people tried to get to Preston and equally interesting to know how many failed to get there in time for the match.

We were travelling to the Old Roan in the time which Colonel Glenn, one of America's spacemen, was orbiting the earth and we heard a broadcast of his progress while on the coach. He circled the earth once while we travelled less than two miles to the Old Roan.

At the Old Roan, the traffic was at a standstill and in the middle of the block was not only our coach, but also our police escort, also jammed.

The position looked so serious that I would have wagered a lot of money that we would never get to Preston the same night. However, in some way, the police managed to free themselves and then get us free.

They did, in fact, escort us to Deepdale, changing the route twice to avoid the heavier traffic and we pulled up at the ground at exactly at the time we should have been kicking off.

The scene on the roads leading to the ground and outside were chaotic. All gates were closed with as many people left outside the ground as had managed to get in.

Old timers in Preston told me that in the long history of their club, they had never witnessed scenes such as this. I think the delay and anxiety over being so late upset the boys a bit; it certainly was not the best approach to a cup tie.

The game was extremely hard-fought and even after extra time, there was no score, but I thought that we might have won the match in extra time. This was not to be and both teams lived to fight again, this time the venue being Old Trafford the following Monday.

We had a league match on the Saturday prior to this against Middlesbrough at home. Conditions were ideal for the game and probably because of this the forwards played their game at a faster pace. Ian St John scored twice and Roger Hunt got another hat-trick.

The Sunday following this game witnessed the same crowd scenes at the ground where tickets for

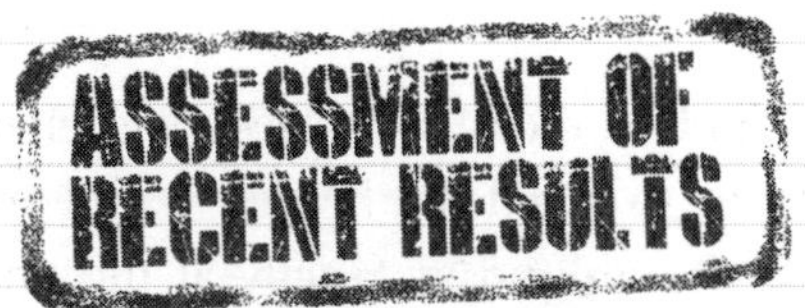

Match summary

Opposition	Comments
10.02.1962 v **Bury** 2nd Div Gigg Lane	Another Hunt hat-trick as we coast through this one-sided contest. Result: Won 3-0
17.02.1962 v **Preston NE** FA Cup 5th rnd Anfield	Surprised and disappointed at result. Bit too sure of ourselves and almost beaten. All to do in the replay. Result: Drew 0-0
20.02.1962 v **Preston NE** FA Cup 5th rnd replay – Deepdale	Chaos! Arrived just in time for kick-off. Game itself hard-fought but again failed to find a winner, even with the addition of extra time. Result: Drew 0-0
24.02.1962 v **Middlesbrough** Second Division Anfield	Fast play from the forwards assured us a comfy win. Another hat-trick for Hunt plus a double from St John. Result: Won 5-1
26.02.1962 v **Preston NE** FA Cup 5th rnd, second replay Old Trafford	Snow and high winds made for tough playing conditions. Solitary goal finally settled tie and although disappointed to exit, we have the league to focus on. Result: Lost 1-0

Monday's second replay were being sold, and it occurred to me that all these games must be proving very expensive to the Liverpool football public, but the queues showed their interest and enthusiasm was boundless.

The game itself was played in Arctic conditions with snow underfoot, snow falling and a high wind which made judgement of a ball in the air extremely difficult. We lost by the only goal scored and so had to bow at the knee of Preston who in all three games had played a rugged type of game.

It would be wrong to suppose that we were not disappointed by our exit from the cup, but because we attached far more importance to winning promotion, this was not as great as it would have been under other circumstances.

A New Signing And Roger's Record

A major event took place before the Middlesbrough match when Jimmy Furnell was signed from Burnley. Although the signing took place on the Friday evening, the news was not made public until the following Monday.

Position: Goalkeeper
Birthplace: Clitheroe
Age: 24yrs 3mnths
Height: 6ft 1ins

Club Career

Burnley: 1954 – present
Debut: Apr 23, 1960 v Blackpool
League Appearances: 2
Goals conceded: 5

Clubs interested...

Everton – Had offer accepted in January
* Player turned down the move

Other notes

* Joined Burnley ground staff in 1954 straight from school, given professional contract on seventeenth birthday

* Currently third-choice keeper behind Colin McDonald and Adam Blacklaw

Expected fee = £15,000–£18,000

APPROVED

This was the player in whom I had been interested in for longer than this particular season and to whom I referred in an earlier article.

He made his debut at Walsall the following week, when we were held to a 1-1 draw. Jimmy made a good impression in his first game and the goal scored against him was from a shot fired when his view was completely blocked by one of our defenders. My official report on him after that match was that "he looked like a goalkeeper."

The following Saturday saw us win comfortably at Anfield with Derby County as our victims and the next week found us away to Leyton Orient. This side, under the management of Johnny Carey, confirmed the impression which I had informed them of earlier in the season and held us to a 2-2 draw.

After this we had a fixture for which the team had eagerly awaited, Preston at Anfield. This was the fifth meeting between the clubs and the boys were still smarting from our defeat at Old Trafford against a club which we had beaten on their own ground.

Nearly 40,000 saw the game and we completely vindicated our honour with a 4-1 win.

We entertained Rotherham United the following Wednesday, a rearranged fixture which had been postponed through the spell of cold weather in January.

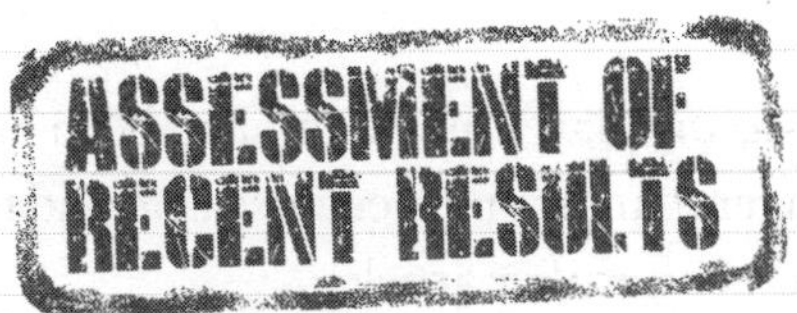

Match summary

Opposition	Comments
03.03.1962 **v Walsal** 2nd Div Fellows Park	Solid debut from Furnell, not at fault for Walsall goal. He looked like a goalkeeper! Result: Drew 1-1
10.03.1962 **v Derby County** Second Division Anfield	Comfortable win; Hunt and Melia both netting doubles, one each in either half. Result: Won 4-1
17.03.1962 **v Leyton Orient** Second Division Brisbane Road	As predicted, another tough encounter with Carey's team. Two goals from A'Court in last 10 minutes helped us to a share of the points. Result: Drew 2-2
24.03.1962 **v Preston NE** Second Division Anfield	Revenge! Restored our honour following epic cup exit. Goals from Melia, St John and two from Hunt, showcased our superiority. Result: Won 4-1
28.03.1962 **v Rotherham** Second Division Anfield	Showed what we can do when this fixture is played under decent conditions! A hat-trick from St John but Hunt scores his 37th goal of the season – a new club record. Result: Won 4-1

ROGER HUNT'S LEAGUE GOALSCORING RECORD

Team	Season	League	Goals	Games	Goals per Game Av.
Roger Hunt	**1961-62***	**Div 2**	**37**	**33**	**1.12**
Gordon Hodgson	1930-31	Div 1	36	40	0.90
Sam Raybould	1902-03	Div 1	31	33	0.94
Jack Parkinson	1909-10	Div 1	30	31	0.97
Gordon Hodgson	1928-29	Div 1	30	38	0.79
Billy Liddell	1954-55	Div 2	30	40	0.75
John Evans	1954-55	Div 2	29	38	0.76
Dick Forshaw	1925-26	Div 1	27	32	0.84
Gordon Hodgson	1934-35	Div 1	27	34	0.79
Billy Liddell	1955-56	Div 2	27	39	0.69
Gordon Hodgson	1931-32	Div 1	26	39	0.67
George Allan	1895-96	Div 2	25	20	1.25
Fred Pagnam	1914-15	Div 1	24	29	0.83
Bobby Robinson	1904-05	Div 2	24	32	0.75
Albert Stubbins	1946-47	Div 1	24	36	0.67
Joe Hewitt	1905-06	Div 1	24	37	0.65
Gordon Hodgson	1932-33	Div 1	24	37	0.65
Gordon Hodgson	1933-34	Div 1	24	37	0.65
Jack Balmer	1946-47	Div 1	24	39	0.62
Albert Stubbins	1947-48	Div 1	24	40	0.60
Jimmy Ross	1895-96	Div 2	23	25	0.92
Gordon Hodgson	1927-28	Div 1	23	32	0.72
Jimmy Smith	1929-30	Div 1	23	37	0.61
Harry Chambers	1922-23	Div 1	22	32	0.69
Billy Liddell	1957-58	Div 12	22	35	0.63
Harry Chambers	1920-21	Div 1	22	40	0.55

* after 4-1 win over Rotherham - 28.03.1962

We had lost to them on an ice-bound pitch and the boys were anxious to show how football should be played under decent conditions. They did; and the margin again was 4-1.

One of the most noteworthy points about this game was that Roger Hunt's goal brought his total for the season to 37, which broke the club's scoring record.

He went on to score another four before the season ended, but Rotherham provided the opposition when the record was broken and the congratulations which he received from his fellow players showed conclusively that they were just as delighted as he was. This is typical of the spirit which exists at Anfield today.

We had now reached the stage in the season when promotion seemed a certainty. We still had eight games to play, we had 52 points and it looked, from the way our nearest rivals' games were coming in, that only one or two more points would make us safe.

This had, of course, been our aim throughout the season, but the target altered slightly at this point. We all felt that, having led the field from the gun, the championship must be our aim and nothing less.

In this frame of mind we visited Luton and played what could be described as a game of missed opportunities. We lost by the only goal, so we were still no nearer our objective.

* * * * *

"It was obvious that supporters merely wanted to chair their heroes around the field: it was equally obvious that Ron Yeats is not the size to be 'chaired' with any ease."

Going Up

The point we earned in a hard match against Huddersfield Town, at Anfield, put us very close indeed to promotion.

However, we had to wait a fortnight before playing again because an outbreak of smallpox in South Wales caused the game which should have been played in Swansea to be postponed.

Making the best of a bad job, I travelled to Glasgow to see the match between Scotland and England in which Ian St John was leading the Scottish attack. Ian had a good game and played a leading part in Scotland's decisive win.

It must be a long time since an international team played with such composure as did Scotland on a bone-hard pitch with the sun beating down mercilessly.

The scenes following the Scottish victory must be unrivalled in Hampden's long history. Players who had partially stripped had hurried to put on some clothing to do a second lap of honour before the crowd would disperse.

Results that day were very much in our favour, for with Scunthorpe beating Leyton and Bury winning at Plymouth, we found that a single point from our next game against Southampton at home would be sufficient to clinch the championship. This, we all felt, should not be beyond our powers.

Forty thousand supporters turned out to see this game on a really terrible day, but surely one of the most memorable in the history of the club.

The only change in the side was one of necessity. Kevin Lewis led the attack instead of the suspended Ian St John and delighted everybody with a first-class display, scoring both the goals which made the margin by which we won.

The scenes which followed the game were quite unprecedented in my experience. The Southampton players honoured us by lining up and applauding the team as they left the field.

It had been the intention for the players to change into a dry strip and after this run a lap of the field as we knew that our supporters would be anxious

SECOND DIVISION
21.04.1962
ANFIELD

Manager		Manager	
Bill Shankly		Edward Bates	
LIVERPOOL	2	SOUTHAMPTON	0
1	Jim Furnell	1	Tony Godfrey
2	Gerry Byrne	2	Roy Patrick
3	Ronnie Moran	3	Tommy Traynor
4	Gordon Milne	4	Ken Wimshurst
5	Ron Yeats	5	Tony Knapp
6	Tommy Leishman	6	Cliff Huxford
7	Ian Callaghan	7	Terry Paine
8	Roger Hunt	8	Brian Clifton
9	Kevin Lewis	9	Derek Reeves
10	Jimmy Melia	10	Tommy Mulgrew
11	Alan A'Court	11	Harry Penk

Goals:- Lewis 19, 29

Attendance:- 40,410

ASSURED OF FIRST DIVISION FOOTBALL NEXT SEASON...

	Team	P	W	D	L	F	A	Pts	GA
1	Liverpool	37	24	7	6	90	35	55	2.57
2	Leyton Orient	40	20	10	10	64	39	50	1.64
3	Sunderland	39	20	8	11	77	49	48	1.57
4	Scunthorpe United	39	20	7	12	82	63	47	1.3
5	Plymouth Argyle	39	19	7	13	73	67	45	1.09
6	Huddersfield Town	39	15	12	12	63	53	42	1.19
7	Southampton	40	17	8	115	71	60	42	1.18
8	Stoke City	39	17	7	15	53	50	41	1.06
9	Rotherham United	39	15	9	15	67	69	39	0.97
10	Bury	40	17	4	19	43	74	38	0.70
11	Newcastle United	40	14	9	17	62	54	37	1.15
12	Luton Town	40	16	4	19	66	68	37	0.97
13	Charlton Athletic	39	14	9	16	66	70	37	0.94
14	Walsall	39	13	11	15	65	69	37	0.94
15	Preston North End	40	14	9	17	52	56	37	0.93
16	Derby County	40	13	11	16	65	73	37	0.89
17	Norwich City	40	13	11	16	57	68	37	0.84
18	Middlesbrough	39	13	7	19	69	70	33	0.99
19	Leeds United	40	11	11	18	49	61	33	0.77
20	Bristol Rovers	40	13	7	11	52	77	33	0.68
21	Brighton & H A	40	10	11	19	42	81	31	0.52
22	Swansea Town	38	10	10	18	51	80	30	0.64

to acknowledge our achievement. However, some of the boys jumped into the bath and as the lap could not be made without a full team, the rest followed their example.

The crowd waited with commendable patience whilst the players cooled off and changed into their ordinary clothes, but the moment Ronnie Yeats showed himself, a tidal wave of humanity surged over the wall of the Kop, swept across the field and engulfed poor Yeats.

Behind Yeats came Ian St John and part of the flood detached itself and completely submerged him.

Other players who were following had the good sense to take refuge in the tunnel, but it was far too late for Yeats and St John to do anything except be carried by their respective tides.

From the stand, the demonstration was frightening. It was obvious that supporters merely wanted to chair their heroes around the field: it was equally obvious that Ron Yeats is not the size to be 'chaired' with any ease.

On the other hand, he is not the size that can easily be put on the ground, even by a mob, and therefore he was just jostled and pushed and pulled with his coat half off, pinioning his arms.

Ian St John was in a far worse plight because of his smaller stature. From time to time he was hoisted aloft and then would suddenly disappear from view. Sometimes only his legs could be seen above the heads of those surrounding him.

Those watching, knowing the enormous pressure that can be exerted by a crowd of this size, were really alarmed for the safety of these players.

Eventually a wedge of very large policemen managed to drive a wedge to Yeats and provide cover while he escaped, and then performed the same office for St John.

In the latter case, the rescue was more than timely because he was nearly black in the face and he said that it seemed he had not been able to breathe for the last 10 minutes.

However, apart from damage to their clothing, no harm was done, both players having undergone their ordeal with good humour and fortitude.

It might have been a good thing if the rest of the boys had joined Yeats and St John, because in this way the crowd would have been dispersed into smaller groups and Ian and Ronnie would not have had to bear the concentration.

Playing Like Champions

This was the proudest moment of my footballing life and I was delighted that I had something to do with the return of Liverpool to First Division football. I was not proud for myself, but proud to be part of a team which had given so much, so consistently, and delighted that the most loyal group of supporters in the game had at last seen their ambition realised.

I suppose that anything after this is an anti-climax. We had five more fixtures to fulfil, but there could never be the same drive and urgency about these that there had been whilst points were a vital necessity. However, we were champions and our idea was to play like champions.

The first of the five was against Stoke City at home, an evening game which was won in the last few seconds with a great goal by Jimmy Meila.

We played the return against this team the next day, which turned out to be a hard, uneventful game as the nil-nil draw suggests, but the same could not be said of our game against Plymouth Argyle on the following Saturday.

Here we were accorded a great welcome as

champions of Division Two, and in spite of playing on a bone-hard pitch with both sides suffering from that end-of-season feeling, the game was a good one and never for a moment lacking interest. We won by the odd goal in five.

The cup tie had dislocated our fixture list and we were in the position now of having to cram many games into a short period. We had played Southampton on the Saturday, Stoke on both Monday and Tuesday, Plymouth on Saturday and were now due to entertain Charlton on Monday.

With commitments as heavy as this, it was with thankfulness and relief that I could regard our unassailable position at the top of the table; a programme of five games in 10 days was one which I would not have liked to have undertaken had there been a championship at stake.

The Charlton match was another memorable affair, and at one time it seemed certain that we would lose our home record.

With a few minutes to go, we were trailing a goal down, but Roger Hunt equalised and I, for one, would have settled for a draw at this point and would have been happy to do so.

The boys, however, had other ideas and Alan A'Court scored the winner in the last few seconds

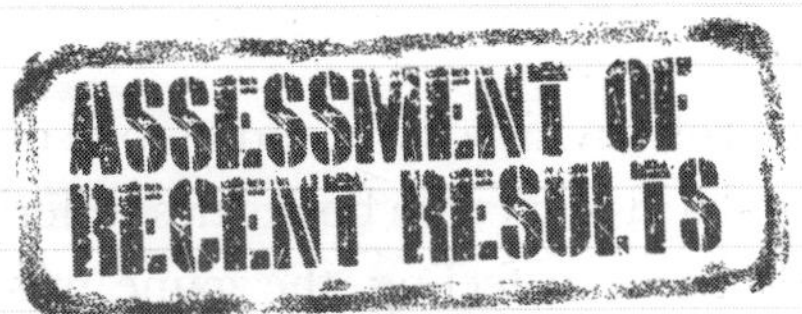

Match summary

Opposition	Comments
23.04.1962 **v Stoke City** Second Division Anfield	First of the back-to-back meetings with Tony Waddington's team went our way thanks to a late strike from Melia. Ronnie Moran had netted our first from the penalty spot in the opening half. Result: Won 2–1
24.04.1962 **v Stoke City** Second Division Victoria Ground	Callaghan came in for Lewis on the right wing in the only change from yesterday's encounter. Not much to note during an uneventful match which ended in a stalemate. Result: Drew 0–0
28.04.1962 **v Plymouth Argyle** Second Division Home Park	Hugely entertaining despite both sides showing end-of-season fatigue. Efforts from A'Court, St John and record-breaking Hunt tipped the five-goal scoreline in our favour. Result: Won 3–2
30.04.1962 **v Charlton Ath** Second Division Anfield	Players showed the fight of true champions when, trailing by a Bailey goal for most of the game, goals from Hunt and A'Court rescued victory in the dying moments. Presented with the league trophy afterwards. Great day! Result: Won 2–1

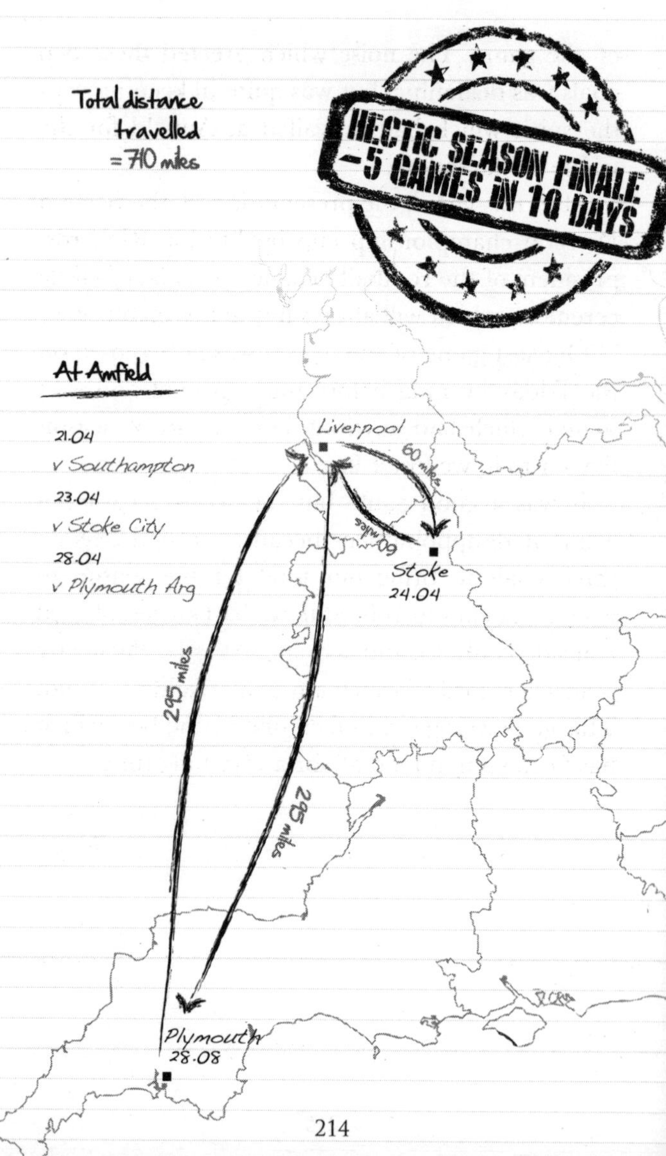
Total distance
travelled
= 710 miles
HECTIC SEASON FINALE
– 5 GAMES IN 10 DAYS
At Anfield
21.04
v Southampton
23.04
v Stoke City
28.04
v Plymouth Arg
Liverpool
60 miles
60 miles
Stoke
24.04
295 miles
295 miles
Plymouth
28.08

of the game. The noise which greeted these two goals was deafening, but was quite in keeping with the spirit which had prevailed at Anfield for the whole of the season.

After this game, the presentation of the Second Division championship cup by Mr Joe Richards, president of the Football League, took place, a little ceremony which will always live in my memory.

Our last game of the season was at Swansea on the Friday evening before the cup final and in a match which had anything but an end of season flavour to it, we lost 4-2.

It was a good game but the score occasioned a minor disappointment because we had needed three goals to bring our total for the season in league matches to 100. Still, we had scored 99 and conceded only 43, and in doing so, had collected 62 points, a record of which any team could be proud. This goal average is, in fact, one of the best which has been seen in football for a very long time.

2ND DIVISION FINAL TABLE 1961/1962...

	Team	P	W	D	L	F	A	Pts	GA
1	Liverpool	42	27	8	7	99	43	62	2.30
2	Leyton Orient	42	22	10	10	69	40	54	1.73
3	Sunderland	42	22	9	11	85	50	53	1.70
4	Scunthorpe United	42	21	7	14	86	71	49	1.21
5	Plymouth Argyle	42	19	8	15	75	75	46	1.00
6	Southampton	42	18	9	15	77	62	45	1.24
7	Huddersfield Town	42	16	12	14	67	59	44	1.14
8	Stoke City	42	17	8	17	55	57	42	0.97
9	Rotherham United	42	16	9	17	70	76	41	0.92
10	Preston North End	42	15	10	17	55	57	40	0.97
11	Newcastle United	42	15	9	18	64	58	39	1.10
12	Middlesbrough	42	16	7	19	76	72	39	1.06
13	Luton Town	42	17	5	20	69	71	39	0.97
14	Walsall	42	14	11	17	70	75	39	0.93
15	Charlton Athletic	42	15	9	18	69	75	39	0.92
16	Derby County	42	14	11	17	68	75	39	0.91
17	Norwich City	42	14	11	17	61	70	39	0.87
18	Bury	42	17	5	20	52	76	39	0.68
19	Leeds United	42	12	12	18	50	61	36	0.82
20	Swansea Town	42	12	12	18	61	83	36	0.74
21	Bristol Rovers	42	13	7	22	53	81	33	0.65
22	Brighton & H A	42	10	11	21	42	86	31	0.49

Goals
0
10
20
30
40
50
Player
A'Court 8
Byrne 1
Callaghan 1
Hunt 41
Leishman 1
Lewis 10
Melia 13
Milne 2
Moran 1
Own Goal 3
St John 18
GOALSCORER CHART
Clean sheets: 12
Average home attendance: 39,227
LEAGUE STATS
GOALS BREAKDOWN
When they went in
Minutes/goals
Average goals scored per game: 2.36
Average goal minute: 50
1–15: 15
16–30: 8
31–45: 15
46–60: 23
61–75: 15
76–90: 23
1–15 15.2%
16–30 8.1%
31–45 15.2%
46–60 23.2%
61–75 15.2%
76–90 23.2%

Paying My Tributes

So ended the memorable season, one full of excitement and it is perhaps appropriate for me to pay tribute to those concerned in the success which we achieved.

First, I would like to thank the chairman and the board for their faith in me and secondly, I must acknowledge the help given by both the office and training staff.

Neither of these branches of the club get the publicity accorded to the players, but without the office staff, matters could not possibly tick smoothly in the way which they do. The training staff have also been wonderful.

It has been the aim at Anfield for the training staff of Reuben Bennett, Bob Paisley and Joe Fagan to read the game as it ebbs and flows and try to find flaws in the opposition with a view to making suggestions at half-time which would be of benefit to the players. Each of these three men has proved his ability in this sphere.

Bob Paisley, because of his association with the first team, has been more closely connected with me throughout the season than the other two and his reading of a game has been of the greatest value on numerous occasions, as has been the case with Reuben Bennett and Joe Fagan with their respective teams.

I also want to thank the players, who gave everything they had in both matches and training, and last but not least, the groundsmen at Anfield and Melwood.

This Is Only The Start

As for myself, I regard our promotion as taking a first step, so that mine is a job only started. The next step is to establish ourselves in Division One.

In this connection we are fortunate in having a comparatively young side and the success achieved last season added to the experience gained will undoubtedly prove a major asset in the future.

Readers of these articles will be aware of my views on physical fitness, opinions vindicated on numerous occasions when superior fitness told its tale in the second half of a hard-fought game.

At the time of writing, the players have completed their preparation for training (training to be fit for training, if you like) and are busy hardening themselves for complete match fitness.

Only the rashest of men (which I am not) would forecast success in the world of football, but any lack of it will not be due to a lack of fitness or endeavour by anybody connected with the Liverpool FC and those thousands of well-wishers will know that they are supporting a team that will always give its best.

I undertook the task of writing this series of articles solely for the benefit of the football public in Liverpool and in them I have given as much detail as possible of events which have taken place since my arrival at Anfield.

My knowledge of the football enthusiast in this city is such that I firmly believe that immediately the last game of one season has been played, he is awaiting the first match of the next with the keenest anticipation.

These are men after my own heart and if my excursion into journalism has given any pleasure to these countless thousands and has helped to pass the time between seasons by reminding them of football occasions and anticipating those which are to come, then I shall have been amply rewarded for my efforts.

In conclusion, I want to give my assurance to all who support Liverpool FC that, in the seasons ahead, we shall always do our utmost to provide good entertainment and good sport.

My task will be to play my part in this endeavour to the best of my ability.

*****

Liverpool Football Club

and Athletic Grounds Co. Ltd.

Manager: W. Shankly
Secretary: J. S. McInnes
Telephone: ANField 2361/2

ANFIELD ROAD
LIVERPOOL · 4

Training Tuesday September 18th 1962.

Warm up 10 minutes.

Four groups.

1.Group.	Five-a-side	(full pitch)
2.Group.	Five-a-side.	(shooting boards)
3.Gropp.	Five-a-side.	(short pitch)
4.Group.		(~~shooting boards~~). Sprinting.

What Happened Next?

It didn't take long for the harsh realities of life back in Division One to hit home.

Shankly remained loyal to the players that had earned Liverpool promotion, but with no new signings brought in that summer, his side found it tough to acclimatise to the top flight.

A 2-1 home defeat to Blackpool on the opening day of the season was a bad start and although there were Anfield victories against Man City, Sheffield United, West Ham and Bolton Wanderers, Liverpool's away form was abysmal, with only two points taken from their opening eight matches on the road.

Ironically, one of those points came from the Merseyside derby that the whole city had been desperate to see – a 2-2 draw at Goodison Park in front of an astonishing crowd of 73,000. Roger Hunt's 90th minute equaliser was celebrated like a cup final winner by Liverpudlians.

But on the night of November 3, after a 2-1 home defeat to Burnley, Liverpool were sat 20th in the league with 11 points, one ahead of Leyton Orient and Ipswich Town in the relegation zone.

A battle to stay up looked likely, but the arrival of left-winger Willie Stevenson from Rangers, the decision to replace keeper Jim Furnell with 22-year-old Tommy Lawrence after a 3-0 reverse at Leicester, plus some straight-talking from Shankly, turned the season around.

"The players got a bit of a complex about this so-called First Division class when they stepped out in the top table," he said. "They've been treating ordinary teams like good teams.

"They got the idea that sides in the First Division must be good. Now they're finding out that isn't always so. There are a lot of ordinary sides in the First Division and Liverpool were far from ordinary when they came into it."

A 2-1 victory against Arsenal, courtesy of a Ronnie Moran penalty, was the catalyst for a run of 11 wins and a draw from 12 games, including four consecutive victories away from home.

Liverpool even found themselves in 4th by the start of March, but their league form fell away as quickly as it had improved with just four victories from the final 17 matches meaning the Reds finished 8th, 17 points behind champions Everton.

A 5-2 Anfield win against Tottenham followed by a 7-2 defeat at White Hart Lane three days later encapsulated how unpredictable Liverpool had become and 8th remains the club's lowest top-flight finish since promotion, equalled only in 1993/94 and 2011/12.

It was an FA Cup run that turned out to be the highlight of Liverpool's season. Victories over Wrexham and Burnley, after a replay, set up a 5th round trip to Highbury where the Reds won 2-1, another Moran penalty being the difference.

Cup fever hit Anfield and a crowd of just under 50,000 saw the Reds beat West Ham 1-0 in the quarter-final, Roger Hunt netting the winner against a side that had Bobby Moore and Martin Peters in its ranks.

Unfortunately, though, Liverpool ran into their bogey-team – Leicester City – in the semi-final and were beaten 1-0 at Hillsborough, meaning dreams of a first ever FA Cup success were over.

But Kopites didn't have to wait long for silverware to be paraded at Anfield again.

Twelve months later, Liverpool were champions of England for the first time since 1947 and a further year down the line the Bill Shankly boys were running round Wembley with the cup after beating Don Revie's Leeds 2-1.

Another league title followed in 1965/66, although a 2-1 defeat to Borussia Dortmund in the European Cup Winners Cup final at Hampden Park prevented a first European trophy being paraded at Anfield.

Further success for Shankly's Liverpool followed in the 1970s, although not before a Wembley cup final defeat to Arsenal in 1971.

Shankly subsequently built a second great Liverpool side and the Reds became champions for the 8th time in 1972/73 and also captured their first piece of European silverware by beating Borussia Moenchengladbach 3-2 on aggregate in the UEFA Cup final.

1973/74 turned out to be Shankly's final season before retirement and he signed off with a second FA Cup success, this time after his side destroyed Newcastle United 3-0 in the final.

By then though, having travelled down the hard road in the early 1960s, Liverpool Football Club were well and truly back.

*****

D.O.B.: 2 Sep, 1913
Birthplace: Glenbuck
Nationality: Scottish

League Honours

2nd Div Champions:
1962
1st Div Champions:
1964, 1966, 1973

Cup Honours

FA Cup Winners:
1965, 1974
UEFA Cup Winners:
1973
Charity Shield:
1964 (shared),
1965 (shared, 1966

OVERALL RECORD

Lost 22.73%
Won 51.98%
Drawn 25.29%

W/L/D Breakdown

Played: 783
Won: 407
Drawn: 198
Lost: 178

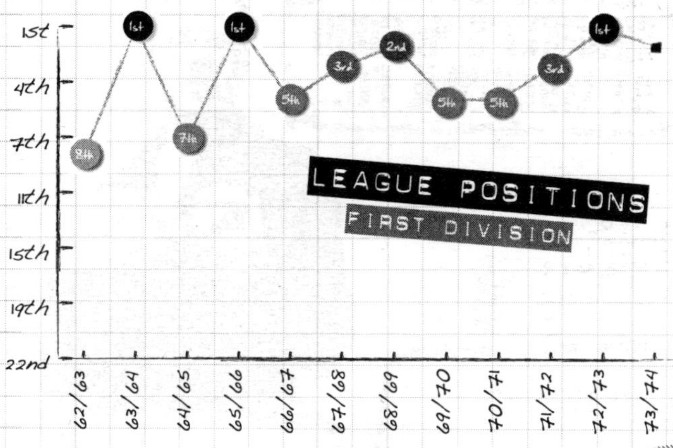

CUP COMPETITIONS

	FA Cup	League Cup	Charity Shield	European Cup	UEFA Cup	ECWC
62/63	SF	-	-	-	-	-
63/64	QF	-	-	-	-	-
64/65	Winners	-	Shared	SF	-	-
65/66	Rnd3	-	Shared	-	-	R-Up
66/67	Rnd5	-	Winners	Rnd2	-	-
67/68	QF	Rnd2	-	-	Rnd3	-
68/69	Rnd5	Rnd4	-	-	Rnd1	-
69/70	QF	Rnd3	-	-	Rnd2	-
70/71	R-up	Rnd3	-	-	SF	-
71/72	Rnd4	Rnd4	-	-	-	Rnd2
72/73	Rnd4	Rnd5	-	-	Winners	-
73/74	Winners	Rnd5	-	Rnd2	-	-

Glossary of Liverpool players

As mentioned by Bill Shankly

Alan A'Court

A tremendous club servant, Rainhill-born Alan A'Court spent over ten years with the club, making his debut as an 18-year-old in 1953. Signed from Prescot Cables, he became a fixture on the left flank at Anfield as the Reds adjusted to life in the Second Division. His performances were good enough to earn selection for the 1958 England World Cup squad. He was a mainstay of the side promoted to the First Division in 1962 but lost his place the following season. His farewell appearance was in the club's first European tie at Anfield against KR Reykjavik in September 1964. He finished his playing career at Tranmere before coaching at Norwich, Crewe and Stoke. He later ran a newsagents in Wirral. A'Court died in 2009, aged 75.

Alf Arrowsmith

A striker recruited from non-league Ashton United in 1960, he first made an impact halfway through the title season of 1963/64, breaking into the team and going on to score 19 times in 24 games. A bad cruciate ligament injury in the 1964 Charity Shield brought his progress to a juddering halt. He was never the same player again and only made occasional first team appearances from then on, eventually departing for Bury in 1968. Arrowsmith died in 2005, aged 62.

John Bennett

A full-back, Bennett was a local lad and signed professional forms but failed to make it to the first team. Aged 20, he moved to Chester City in the summer of 1966 and after three years at Sealand Road, he moved to non-league Macclesfield Town. He was part of the Macclesfield side who won the first FA Trophy with a 2-0 defeat of Telford in 1970.

Gerry Byrne

A one-club man, left-back Byrne will always be associated with the 1965 FA Cup final where he played the whole game, plus extra-time, with a broken collarbone sustained in the third minute (substitutes were not permitted until 1967). A courageous, selfless act that was pivotal to the Reds bringing home the cup for the first time – he provided the cross for Roger Hunt to open the scoring in extra-time. A Liverpool lad, Byrne had made his debut as a 19-year-old in 1957 and went on to win two league championship medals with Liverpool, being ever-present in 1965/66 and the Second Division promotion campaign of 1961/62. He made his 333rd and final Reds appearance in 1969.

Ian Callaghan

Another Liverpool legend, Callaghan stands alone with 857 appearances for the club, a record that will surely never be beaten. After making his debut, aged 18, towards the end of the 1959/60 season, he was virtually a fixture in the side for almost two decades, spending the first half of his career on the right wing before being moved inside by Bill Shankly following a knee operation. After being part of the promotion side, Cally won two league championship medals and the FA Cup in the 1960s and was still a key figure when Liverpool began hoovering up trophies at home and abroad from 1973. He was in the starting XI for the first European Cup win in Rome in 1977 and an unused substitute for the Wembley final against Bruges 12 months later. He joined Swansea City in 1978, ending his playing career with Crewe Alexandra in 1982, days before his 40th birthday. He later worked in insurance and joined the pools panel alongside former team-mate Roger Hunt.

Jimmy Furnell

Signed from Burnley in 1962, goalkeeper Furnell almost immediately displaced Bert Slater and played the final 13 fixtures of that promotion season. With Liverpool back in the First Division, Furnell continued in goal until he broke a finger in training in October. He was replaced by Tommy Lawrence and never played for the Reds again. He left for Arsenal the following year and was their first choice 'keeper for five years until Bob Wilson took over. He finished his playing career at Rotherham United and Plymouth Argyle.

Bobby Graham

Recruited from Motherwell Bridge Works youth team, Graham graduated from the reserves in 1964/65 and arrived in style – scoring on his first-team debut as Anfield hosted European football for the first time and KR Reykjavik were beaten 5–0. Graham then scored a hat-trick in his league debut, a 5-1 win over Aston Villa, 12 days later. He scored in the following game too, but didn't maintain the momentum and played only occasionally for the rest of the decade. However, as Ian St John and Roger Hunt fell out of favour, he was ever-present in the 1969/70 season. In October 1970, a broken leg sustained against Chelsea painfully halted his progress. The arrival of John Toshack and, soon after, Kevin Keegan meant he fell down the pecking order. He scored on his final Reds appearance in 1972 and left for Coventry City, before heading home and playing for Motherwell and Hamilton Academical.

Jimmy Harrower

Signed by Phil Taylor from Hibernian in January 1958, aged 22, Harrower was a skilful attacking midfielder but one prone to inconsistency. He battled for the inside-left position with Jimmy Melia for a time but Melia eventually prevailed and Harrower joined Newcastle. After a short stay on Tyneside, he signed for Falkirk, returning to his native Scotland where he spent the rest of his career. He died in 2006.

Dave Hickson

Hickson had a short but significant impact at Anfield when he made a controversial switch from Everton in November 1959, shortly before Shankly took over. He scored twice on his debut as the Reds defeated Aston Villa 2-1. He scored 21 in total that season and another 17 in 1960/61 as his all-action style won over the fans. He left in the summer of 1961 as Ian St John was brought in.

Roger Hunt

'Sir Roger' remains Liverpool's greatest goalscorer in league matches, netting 245 times in 404 appearances between 1959 and 1969. Only Ian Rush has scored more in all competitions. Signed from Stockton Heath in 1958, he made a goalscoring debut against Scunthorpe in September 1959 and swiftly made a name for himself, scoring 21 league goals and two in the FA Cup. Ian St John's arrival in 1961 helped establish one of the most successful striking partnerships in the club's history – one that endured for the rest of the '60s. Hunt scored 41 times from 41 games, including five hat-tricks. Hunt was Liverpool's top scorer every season from 1961/62 to 1968/69 and scored the opening goal as the FA Cup was won for the first time in 1965. His glorious career at Anfield came to an end in 1969/70 when he joined Bolton. After his playing career ended, Hunt worked for the pools panel.

Chris Lawler

A calm, composed defender who popped up time and again with crucial goals, netting 61 times in 549 appearances over 12 years. A local lad, he signed a professional contract on his 17th birthday in October 1960. He had to wait until 1963 for his debut. He became a regular in the 1964/95 season at right-back, and made 316 consecutive appearances between October 1965 and April 1971, and was again ever-present as the league title and UEFA Cup were won in 1972/73. A serious knee injury sustained at QPR in November '73 was the beginning of the end of his Liverpool career and he was only chosen intermittently after that. He left for Portsmouth in October 1975. He later coached Liverpool's reserves but Kenny Dalglish replaced him with Phil Thompson in 1986.

Tommy Leishman

One of many Scots at Anfield during this era, Leishman was recruited from St Mirren shortly before Bill Shankly's arrival. A wing-half, he barely missed a match over the next two-and-a-half years but lost his place to Willie Stevenson early in the 1962/63 season, when the Reds had returned to the First Division. He returned to Scotland to sign for Hibernian in January 1963, later joining Irish league Linfield as player-manager and being named Ulster Footballer of the Year in 1965/66.

Kevin Lewis

The winger's Liverpool career lasted only three years but he made quite an impact, averaging better than a goal every other game. From Ellesmere Port, he was recruited from Sheffield United in June 1960. In his first season he scored three more goals than Roger Hunt. Despite his prolific form, he lost his place to Ian Callaghan but came to score both goals as the Reds clinched promotion with a 2-0 win over Southampton in April 1962. He switched wings with Liverpool back in the First Division, displacing Alan A'Court, and scored in the first Merseyside league derby for over ten years. However, Peter Thompson's arrival in '63 hastened his exit and he joined Huddersfield Town. Before long he moved to South Africa where he settled after a knee injury finished his career at 28.

Billy Liddell

One of the greatest players to ever wear the red shirt, Liddell's Liverpool career was winding down when Shankly took over as manager but his deeds were already enshrined in legend. Signed from Lochgelly Viollet in 1938, his first-team debut was delayed until January 5, 1946 (five days before his 24th birthday) by the outbreak of war. Initially a winger before moving to centre-forward, Liddell still managed to make 534 appearances for the club, then a record, scoring 228 goals. His all-round brilliance was a shining light during a period when Liverpool were in the doldrums, with the league title of 1946/47 the only honour won by the Reds within his career span. His final appearance came in August 1960. He had already become a magistrate by this point and was bursar at the University of Liverpool. He died in 2001, aged 79.

Jimmy Melia

Jimmy Melia was very much a local hero. Brought up in the Scotland Road district of Liverpool, he was captain of Liverpool Schools and signed a professional contract on his 17th birthday in 1954. An inside-left, he scored on his debut in 1955 and became a regular while still a teenager. He was top scorer in the 1958/59 season and Bill Shankly identified him as one of the club's key players when he took over in the closing days of the decade. Melia played in every game of the 1961/62 promotion season, but an injury in December 1963 all but ended his Liverpool career, as he lost his place to Alf Arrowsmith. After three further appearances, he left for Wolverhampton Wanderers in March 1964. Although he missed out on the league title celebrations, Melia had made enough appearances to earn a championship medal. His playing career wound down at Southampton, Aldershot and Crewe before he became a manager, memorably taking Brighton to the 1983 FA cup final and knocking out Liverpool along the way. After coaching in the United Arab Emirates, Portugal and Kuwait, Melia settled in America, coaching youth teams in Texas before re-establishing his connection to his boyhood club by being appointed technical director of Liverpool FC America Youth Soccer.

Gordon Milne

A right-half and fine servant of the club, Milne came from Preston in 1960 and settled quickly, going on to form an effective partnership with Gerry Byrne. He was key to the promotion campaign and two league titles but sadly missed out on the 1965 FA Cup final because of injury. Famously, he and Byrne paraded the trophy to the Anfield crowd before the European Cup semi-final with Inter Milan days later. He left for Blackpool in 1967 before embarking on a long and varied managerial career, taking charge of Wigan Athletic, Coventry City, Leicester City, Besiktas, Nagoya Grampus Eight, Bursapor and Trabzonspor. He was also director of football at Newcastle when Sir Bobby Robson was manager.

Johnny Molyneux

A right-back recruited from Chester in 1955, Molyneux was a dependable presence in the late 1950s before losing his place in the promotion campaign of 1961/62 after Ron Yeats' arrival led to Dick White being moved from centre-half to Molyneux's position. He returned to Chester in 1962.

Ronnie Moran

Moran is generally known as one of the Boot Room boys, but he was a significant figure within the Reds' side in the 1950s and early '60s. An apprentice electrician who began playing with the Liverpool 'C' team, he became established at left-back in the 1954/55 season and was later appointed club captain by Phil Taylor. Although Bill Shankly gave the armband to Dick White and then Ron Yeats, Moran was still part of the side in the promotion campaign and when the First Division title was won in 1963/64. He lost his place in the side the following season and made his final first-team appearances in the European Cup semi-finals against Inter Milan. A year later he was invited to the join the backroom team by Bill Shankly, acting as the 'sergeant major' under, successively, Shankly, Bob Paisley, Joe Fagan, Kenny Dalglish, Graeme Souness and Roy Evans. He was twice caretaker manager, firstly following Kenny Dalglish's shock resignation in February 1991 and while Graeme Souness was recuperating from heart surgery towards the end of the 1991/92 season. Moran led the Liverpool team out at Wembley before the victorious 1992 FA Cup final against Sunderland.

Johnny Morrissey

Morrissey's name is more associated with feats achieved on the other side of Stanley Park but it was at Liverpool he started his career. An uncompromising but brilliant midfielder, Morrissey's opportunities at Anfield were limited by the presence of Alan A'Court and he was sold by the club's board to Everton in 1962, much to Bill Shankly's fury and the Reds boss offered his resignation. He scored on his Everton debut – against Liverpool.

Joseph Parley

A talented centre-back and right-back, Parley was still part of the Liverpool squad in the 1965/66 season but never progressed beyond the reserve side. After leaving the Reds, he is believed to have worked in the car sales business.

Sammy Reid

Reid is most notable for being Bill Shankly's first signing as Liverpool manager, brought in from Motherwell in February 1960. The winger never made a first-team appearance and later that year moved to Falkirk. He later played for Clyde and, after a serious knee injury, joined part-time Berwick Rangers for whom he scored a memorable Scottish Cup winner against Rangers in 1967. In an interview in August 2012, he quipped: "I was Bill Shankly's first signing for Liverpool, although I wasn't there long enough to find out where the River Mersey was."

George Scott

Scott was a Scot. Signed as a youth played aged 15 in 1960, he shared lodgings with Bobby Graham and Gordon Wallace, who would be team-mates, along with Tommy Smith and Chris Lawler, in the Liverpool reserve side. He was a regular scorer for the second-string but never made a first-team breakthrough. He was sold to his hometown club, Aberdeen, in 1965, and scored on his debut in a 2-0 victory over Glasgow Rangers. After a serious knee injury, he played in South Africa before returning to Merseyside and joining Tranmere Rovers. After his football career, Scott had a number of managerial jobs working in sales for companies such as Nestle and United Co-operative Health Care Group.

Bert Slater

A goalkeeper signed from Falkirk in 1959, Slater had a difficult start to his Liverpool career as he conceded eight goals in his first three appearances. Despite the Reds winning two of those games, he was dropped before regaining the position shortly before Shankly's arrival. After 96 consecutive league matches, Slater lost out to Jim Furnell in March 1962 and never played for the first team again. He left for Dundee that summer, who were then managed by Bob Shankly, Bill's older brother. He moved back south three years later to join Watford Later in life he was involved in golf course design. He died in 2006, aged 70.

Tommy Smith

The formidable Anfield Iron is one of the most iconic figures to ever wear the red shirt. Making his first-team debut towards the end of the 1962/63 season, he initially played up front but was moved back into the centre of defence in 1964 and here he remained for the majority of his hugely successful career. He barely missed a game – or a tackle – over the next ten years. Once in his 30s, he featured more often at right-back while also offering cover in all defensive positions. The 1976/77 season was meant to be his last and the European Cup final in Rome against Borussia Moenchengladbach loomed as his final match. His superb header from a corner gave the Reds a 2-1 lead which Phil Neal extended with a late penalty. It was the ultimate achievement for Liverpool fans as they conquered Europe for the first time. In the event, Smith stayed for another season and only an injury sustained while gardening prevented him from playing in the 1978 final against Bruges. His playing career ended at Swansea City and, in retirement, he has been a long-time columnist for the Liverpool Echo.

Ian St John

A club legend, St John helped transform Liverpool when Shankly recruited him and Ron Yeats in 1961. After scoring a hat-trick on his debut in the Liverpool Senior Cup final against Everton, St John took the Second Division by storm as he struck up an attacking partnership with Roger Hunt that sustained the Reds through the decade. Promotion was achieved in their first campaign together and a first championship in 27 years came in 1963/64. Famously, St John scored the winner with a diving header as the FA Cup was won for the first time in 1965. The Scot's pugnacious approach, tactical brain and bravery made him a firm favourite with the fans and he was key to another league title in 1969. When Shankly revamped the team at the dawn of the 1970s, St John fell out of favour and saw out his playing career with Hellenic in South Africa, Coventry City and Tranmere Rovers. He tried club management but it was in television where he enjoyed a successful media career, appearing regularly on ITV for 20 years. He continues to broadcast for Radio City in Liverpool.

Phil Tinney

A midfielder, Tinney was said to have played football in Holland before moving across the pond to take part in the North American Soccer League in the late 1960s and early 1970s, representing the Philadelphia Spartans in 1967 and Dallas Tornado between 1970 and 1972.

Alex Totten

From Stirlingshire, Totten signed a youth contract with Liverpool straight from school but never broke into the first team with the Reds. That didn't stop him having a lengthy playing and managerial career, though. In 1964, when still a teenager, he headed back to Scotland and joined Dundee, going on to represent Dunfermline Athletic, Falkirk, Queen of the South and Alloa Athletic. He then managed Alloa and Falkirk before becoming Jock Wallace's assistant with Glasgow Rangers, leaving Ibrox in 1986 when Graeme Souness was appointed manager. Totten was back as boss with Dumbarton before a five-year spell with St Johnstone from 1987-92 during which he led them from the old Second Division to the Premier Division. After managing East Fife and Kilmarnock, he returned to Falkirk in 1996 and guided the Bairns to the 1997 Scottish Cup final, which they lost to his previous club Kilmarnock. Falkirk met Rangers in a testimonial match for him in 2007. In a 2005 interview, Totten said: "'Bill Shankly was my first manager and he left a huge impression on me. It didn't matter if you were a youth-team player or a top team star. Shankly treated everyone exactly the same and it created a great atmosphere at the club. I like to think I took some of his methods into my own career as a manager."

Gordon Wallace

An inside-left, Wallace, another Scot, is particularly notable for scoring Liverpool's first European goal in August 1964 and, five days later, netting twice when Liverpool beat Arsenal 3-2 in the first game to be shown on the BBC's 'Match of the Day'. Despite this, he was unable to sustain a first-team place and departed for Crewe Alexandra in 1967. Post-football, he settled in Liverpool and was captain of West Derby Golf Club in 2008.

Johnny Wheeler

A Crosby lad, Wheeler's professional career began at Tranmere Rovers in the Third Division North. He then moved to Bolton Wanderers and featured in the famous 'Matthews' FA Cup final in 1953. In 1956 he joined Liverpool and, in only his fourth league appearance, the wing-half scored a hat-trick against Port Vale with goals coming in the 81st, 82nd and 85th minutes. Wheeler was appointed captain by Phil Taylor two years later. He lost his place to Gordon Milne in the early 1960s and his Reds career came to an end. He was appointed player-manager of New Brighton in 1963 but did not take up the position, instead working for Bury as assistant trainer.

Dick White

Signed from hometown club Scunthorpe by Don Welsh in 1955, it took until 1957/58 before White was an established presence in the Liverpool team. Ron Yeats' arrival in 1961 precipitated a move to right-back at the start of the 1961/62 season, but White lost the captaincy and his place halfway through the campaign when Gerry Byrne took over the number 2 shirt. He joined Doncaster in 1962, became player-manager at Kettering Town and later bought a motor business in Nottingham. He died in 2002, aged 70.

Ron Yeats

The famous 'Colossus' was signed from Dundee United in the summer of 1961 and it wasn't long before Bill Shankly appointed him captain in succession to Dick White, handing him the armband for a Boxing Day match against Rotherham United. When promotion was sealed with a win against Southampton in April 1962, Yeats was engulfed by the Liverpool fans and reportedly ended up in the boys' pen. He lifted two First Division titles in 1964 and 1966 but perhaps his crowning achievement was skippering the first FA Cup-winning side in 1965. He formed a formidable central defensive partnership with Tommy Smith before losing his place to Larry Lloyd in 1970, leaving the following year to join Tranmere Rovers as player-manager. In 1986, after a spell away from football, he returned to Liverpool as chief scout and continued in that role under successive managers until retiring 20 years later.

*****

OTHER SPORT MEDIA TITLES

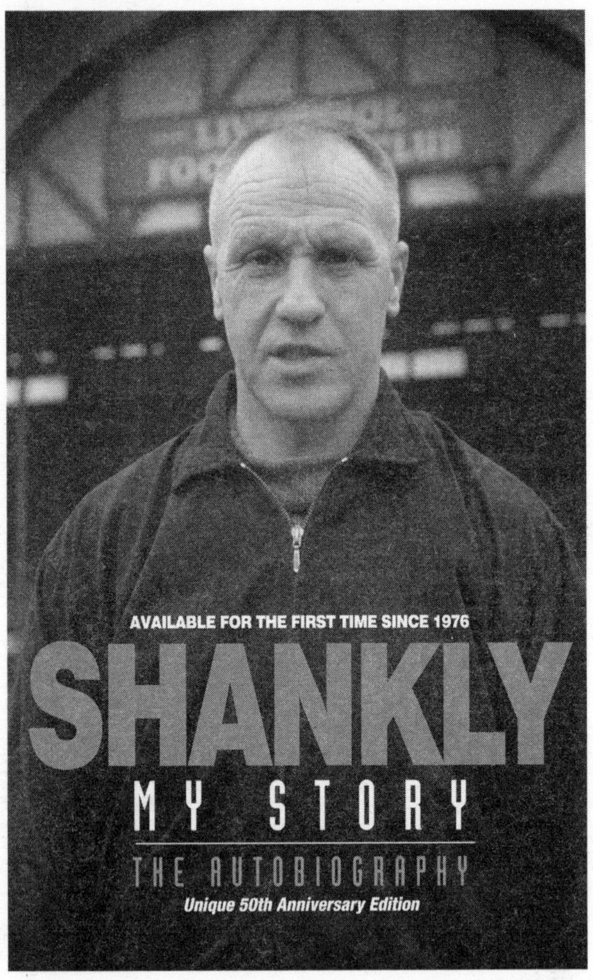

AVAILABLE TO ORDER BY CALLING 0845 143 0001
OR PURCHASE ONLINE AT **WWW.MERSEYSHOP.COM**